An Introduction to Intellectual Property Rights

An Introduction to Intellectual Property Rights

Manju Pathak
Professor of Biotechnology
Amity University
Noida, Uttar Pradesh
India.

NEW INDIA PUBLISHING AGENCY
New Delhi – 110 034

NEW INDIA PUBLISHING AGENCY
101, Vikas Surya Plaza, CU Block, LSC Market
Pitam Pura, New Delhi 110 034, India
Phone: + 91 (11)27 34 17 17 Fax: + 91(11) 27 34 16 16
Email: info@nipabooks.com
Web: www.nipabooks.com

Feedback at feedbacks@nipabooks.com

ISBN : 978-93-83305-12-4

Composed and Designed by NIPA

Dedication

This book is dedicated to my Mother, who has ever till now been my inspiration.

Preface

I entered in teaching profession in year 2008. Apart from teaching courses in Cell Biology and Genetics, I used to take classes for Intellectual Property Rights. It's interesting to see that our undergraduate and postgraduate courses' syllabi includes core course on IPR. This subject, as I see it, is the need of the present time and I think the wealth of the intellectuals, particularly in India, has to be utilized for the development of self, nation and globe at large. The purpose of writing this book is to make available a textbook in IPR for all college and university students. I maintain that the course on IPR should be introduced in early school levels so that our children should know about the legal protection of their intellectual wealth much earlier than what we came across.

I have written this book keeping the syllabus of the subject "IPR" in mind but this would be useful for the general public also. I appreciate any feedbacks from students and instructors that may be delivered directly to me electronically at *patmanju11@gmail.com*

Manju Pathak

Acknowledgments

I acknowledge my students who showed their need of study material all the time in IPR which inspired me to write a book.

Manju Pathak

Contents

Dedication .... *v*
Preface .... *vii*
Acknowledgement .... *ix*

1. Introduction to IPR 1
- 1.1 General Introduction, History, Ownership of Tangible and Intellectual Property 1
- 1.2 Patentable Subject Matter 4
- 1.3 Basic Requirements of Patentability 5
- 1.4 Novelty, Public Domain, Obviousness and Non Obviousness 7
- 1.5 Inventive Step (Non-Obviousness) and Industrial Application 8

2. Patent Specification Drafting 17
- 2.1 Specification Drafting 17
- 2.2 Methods and Precautions in Drafting Patent Specification 18
- 2.3 Disclosure Requirements 21
- 2.4 Patent Claims 21
- 2.5 Filing of A Patent Application 22

3. IPR Issues 25
- 3.1 Competitive and Collaborative Research 25
- 3.2 The Strategy to Protecting Plants : Plant Variety Protection Act 27
- 3.3 IPR Issues in Biotechnological Patents Haldi, Neem and Basmati Rice 32
- 3.4 Patent Litigation 34

4. Patent Applications 39
- 4.1 Provisional and Complete Specifications 39

4.2 Publication 45
4.3 Request of Examination 45
4.4 PCT Application: Gateway to Foreign Patents 48

5. Patent Bodies 51

5.1 TRIPS 51
5.2 WTO 53
5.3 WIPO 54
5.4 Paris Convention 59
5.5 Berne Convention 60
5.6 Budapest Treaty 62
5.7 Madrid Agreement Marks (MAM) 65
5.8 The Patent Law Treaty (PLT) 68

6. Other Fields of Intellectual Property Protection 71

6.1 Copyrights 71
6.2 Trademarks 76
6.3 Geographical Indications 79
6.4 Trade Secrets 81

7. Appendix A: *Diagrammatic Presentation of Processes Involved in Obtaining an Indian Patent 83*

8. Appendix B: *References 85*

Chapter - 1

Introduction to IPR

1.1 General Introduction, Ownership of Tangible and Intellectual Property

Intellectual Property Rights (IPR) are the rights acquired by an individual or a group of individuals through the government over creation of mind. It can be patents, copyrights, trademarks or geographical indications. They are territorial rights except copyright. As creation of mind has a wide spectrum so are the various types of IPRs. It can be a process, product, design, literature, music, art, computer programs or a brand name. The essential requirement for all types of Intellectual Property (IP) is that it should be *Novel*.

People gather money through various means and buy property which is tangible but thinkers produce ideas and make it functional, researchers observe the technicalities involved in the nature and add new dimensions to it and make it more useful for the society. These creations do not fetch them money but people who use their research and are able to market their research earn a lot and create tangible property. Finally creators remain deprived of benefits as for manufacturing and marketing one' requires money which he lacks. The reason being that researcher never worked for money he worked for knowledge. Many researchers require expenditure of huge amount of money, in the absence of IPR by the inventor/s the commercial benefit of research can be enjoyed by anybody and finally the original inventor/s will suffer financially. Therefore IPR provides impetus to the inventors to spend large amount of money in carrying out research.

Thinking upon these circumstances the concept of IPR was first introduced in United Kingdom in seventeenth century. The first legislation in India relating to patents was the Act VI of 1856. The Act was subsequently repealed by Act IX of 1857 and then by XV of 1859. In 1911, the Indian Patents and Design Act, 1911(Act II of 1911) was brought in replacing all the previous legislations on patents and designs. Through this Act for the first time patent administration was brought under the management of Controller of Patents. This Act was amended in 1920 to allow entering into reciprocal arrangements with UK and other countries for securing priority (priority is the date of first filing of patent application). In 1930 it was again amended to incorporate provisions for the grant of patent of additions, secret patents and use of patents by government. In 1945 a major amendment was done about filing of provisional submission and submission of complete submission within nine months. After independence, in 1949, Government of India constituted a committee under chairmanship of Justice Dr Bakshi Tek Chand, a retired judge of Lahore High Court. This committee ensured that patent system should be conducive for a national interest. Based on the recommendations of the committee the 1911 Act was again amended in 1950 (XXXII of 1950). In 1957, the Government of India appointed a committee chaired by Justice N. Rajagopala Aayangar to examine questions of revision of the patent law and advise government. On his recommendations many modifications and revisions were done in the Act and then a patent Act 1970 was passed. This Act repealed and replaced the 1911 Act so far as the patents law is concerned. For designs though the Act of 1911 continued to be applicable. Most of the provisions of the 1970 Act were brought into force on 20th April, 1972 with the publications of the Patents Rules, 1972. The salient features of 1970 Act were: No product patents for substances intended to be used as food, drugs and medicines including the product of chemical substances, elaborate definition of Invention, codification of certain inventions as non-patentable, adoption of absolute novelty criteria in case of publication, enlargement on the grounds for revocation of a patents and additional powers to Central

Government to use an invention for purposes of government including Government undertakings.

This Act remained in force for about 24 years till December 1994 without any change. First amendment to this Act was done in 1995 (which allowed filing of product patents in area of drugs, pharmaceuticals and agro; however such applications were to be examined only after 31st December 2004), second amendment was done in 2002 (20 year term for all patents were introduced) and third amendment was done in 2005. Third amendment introduced product patents to all fields of technology including food, drugs and microorganisms. This right was given to the creators by the government. Hence these IP can be rented out (licensed) or can be sold (sale of IP). The last amendments were effective from 5th May 2006. These rights were exclusively given to inventors/creators/authors for exclusive manufacturing and marketing. The creations were categorized in various classes and accordingly IPR was granted to them. Obviously many of these properties were intangible which you cannot touch or see. This Intellectual Property is very different from tangible properties in nature but can generate money like them. The IPR is a property which fulfills the meaning of property in true sense. Ownership of property in means highest right man can have. The IP not only enriches the Inventor/creator but also strengthens the economy of the country. This economy is knowledge based economy which is a vicious circle between inventor, businessman, society and government. Government earns money from IP fees and after grant maintenance fee. The inventor earns royalty by licensing the IP or huge money by selling the IP; the business person who acquires IP earns by selling the product in the market and this is how money keeps on flowing. Besides IP's contribution to economy it enriches technical knowhow of society and the technology also enriches due to lucrative rights given under IP. IP is country based and hence to explore the business in foreign country IP of that country has to be acquired. Also it is necessary that the individual should file the IP application in one's own country first before moving to the foreign territories. Patent system in India is administered under the Controller General of Patents, Designs and Trademarks (CGPDTM). The office of CGPDTM is subordinate office of Department of Industrial Policy and Promotion under the Ministry of Commerce and Industry. The Controller General´s office is located at Mumbai. There are four patent offices in India. The Head office is at Kolkata and other offices are located in Delhi, Chennai and Mumbai. The Controller General of Patents, Designs and Trademarks delegates his powers for various procedural requirements to Joint Controller, Deputy Controller and Assistant Controllers of Patents and Designs.

1.2 Patentable Subject Matter

In this heading patentable subject matter will be discussed. Different creations are protected with different IP. What can be protectable by patents cannot be protectable by copyrights and vice versa but sometimes to have complete protection for the creation various types of IP are secured to have complete protection. Any process, product or design which is novel, has inventive step and holds industrial application is termed as **Invention** and is **patentable**. Individual who creates is called as **Inventor.** Invention has to be new and capable of being made or used in Industry. **Inventive step** is the technical contribution of the inventor to the prior art causing technical enhancement in the existing process or the product making it **Novel**. **Novelty** is defined as any process or product not known in any form and is neither obvious to lay man or the person skilled in the art. **New Invention** thereby means any technology or invention which has not been anticipated by publication in any document or used in any form in any country of the world before the date of filing of patent application with complete specification. This means that the subject matter under patent has not fallen in public domain in any form. A patent is granted for an **Invention.** An Invention is defined in section 2(1) (j) as "a new product or process involving an inventive step. A patent grants an exclusive manufacturing and marketing right for an invention to the Inventor for a limited time period; which is presently twenty years. A patentee avails the exclusive right to prevent a third party from making, using, marketing, selling or importing the patented product or process within the country during the term of patent. To keep patent in working condition the prescribed maintenance fee should be paid to patent office in time. The patent Act is also called as the Patents Act, 1970. The Patent Act is applicable to whole India. The patent granted in India provides rights of exclusive manufacturing and marketing only in Indian Territory and valid only in India, though nobody can file for IPR on the same invention as it is disclosed and novelty is overcome. **Inventive step** means any technological enhancement in prior art i.e. pre-existing knowledge, or having economic significance or both which is not obvious to lay man or the person skilled in the art. Therefore the criteria for an invention to be patentable are:- 1) it must be Novel 2) it must have an inventive step 3) it must be capable of industrial application. Further invention should not fall under any of the categories of "Inventions Not Patentable" mentioned under sections (3) and (4) of the Patent Act 1970.

An invention to be considered new should not have been published anywhere in the world or not known in any form like local indigenous knowledge or in stories. In brief the invention has not fallen in the public domain or that it does not form part of the state of the art before the date of filing of patent application. In order to establish the Novelty of the invention search for previous publication and by prior claim in any patent application in relation to the subject matter of the invention is conducted by the examiner. Novelty is determined before inventive step because the creative contribution of the inventor can be assessed only by knowing the novel elements of the invention. An invention defined in the claim lacks novelty if the specified combinations of the features have already been anticipated in a previous disclosure. In order to say lack of novelty, the anticipatory disclosure must be contained within a single document.

1.3 Basic Requirements of Patentability

A patent is a document, issued, upon application, by a government office (or a regional office acting for several countries), which describes an invention and creates a legal situation in which the patented invention can normally only be exploited (manufactured, used, sold, imported) with the authorization of the owner of the patent. "Invention" means a solution to a specific problem in the field of technology. An Invention may relate to a product or process. The protection conferred by the patent is limited in time (generally 20 years). Patents are frequently referred to as "monopolies" but the patent does not give the right to the inventor or the owner of a patented invention to make, use or sell anything. The effects of the grant of a patent are that the patented invention may not be exploited in the country by persons other than the owner of the patent unless the owner agrees to such exploitation. Thus, while the owner is not given a statutory right to practice his invention, he is given a statutory right to prevent others from commercially exploiting his invention, which is frequently referred to as a right to exclude others from making, using or selling the invention. The right to take action against any person exploiting the patented invention in the country without his agreement constitutes the patent owner's most important right, since it permits him to derive the material benefits to which he is entitled as a reward for his intellectual effort and work, and compensation for the expenses which his research and experimentation leading to the invention have entailed. However, that while the country may grant patent rights, it does not automatically enforce them, and it is up to the owner of a patent to bring an action, usually under civil law, for any infringement of his patent rights.

An invention must meet several criteria if it is to be eligible for patent protection. These include, most significantly, that the invention must consist of patentable subject matter, the invention must be industrially applicable (useful), it must be new (novel), it must exhibit a sufficient "inventive step" (be non-obvious), and the disclosure of the invention in the patent application must meet certain standards. In order to be eligible for patent protection, an invention must fall within the scope of patentable subject matter. Patentable subject matter is established by statute, and is usually defined in terms of the exceptions to patentability, the general rule being that patent protection shall be available for inventions in all fields of technology (Article 27.1 of the TRIPS Agreement).

Fields of technology which are excluded from the scope of patentable subject matter includes the following:

- discoveries of materials or substances already existing in nature;
- scientific theories or mathematical methods;
- plants and animals other than microorganisms, and essentially biological processes for the production of

plants and animals, other than non-biological and microbiological processes;

- schemes, rules or methods, such as those for doing business, performing purely mental acts or playing games;
- methods of treatment for humans or animals, or diagnostic methods practiced on humans or animals (but not products for use in such methods).

The TRIPS Agreement (Article 27.2) further specifies that Members may exclude from patent protection certain kinds of inventions, for instance inventions the commercial exploitation of which would contravene public order or morality.

1.4 Novelty, Public Domain, Obviousness and Non Obviousness

Novelty

Novelty is an undisputed condition of patentability. Novelty is not something which can be proved or established; only its absence can be proved. It should be noted that in considering novelty, it is not permissible to combine separate items of prior art together.

Public Domain (Prior Art)

An invention is new if it is not anticipated by the prior art. "Prior art" is, in general, all the knowledge that existed prior to the relevant filing or priority date of a patent application, whether it existed by way of written or oral disclosure in public globally.

The disclosure of an invention so that it becomes part of the prior art may take place in three ways, namely: Through publication (by a description of the invention in a published writing or publication in other form like pictures), spoken words uttered in public, such a disclosure being called an oral disclosure or by the use of the invention in public, or by putting the public in a position that enables any member of the public to use it, such a disclosure being a "disclosure by use." Publication in tangible form requires that there be some physical carrier for the information, a document in the broad sense of the term, and that document must have been published, that is to say, made available in the public domain in any manner such as by offering for sale or deposit in a public collection. Publications include issued patents or published patent applications, writings (whether they be manuscript, typescript, or printed matter), pictures including photographs, drawings or films, and recording, whether they be discs or tapes in either spoken or coded language. Today, publication on the Internet must increasingly be taken into consideration. Oral disclosure, as the expression suggests, implies that the words or form of the disclosure are not necessarily recorded as such and includes lectures and radio broadcasts. Disclosure by use is essentially a public, visual disclosure such as by display, sale, demonstration, unrecorded television broadcasts and actual public use. A document will only destroy the novelty of any invention claimed if the subject matter is explicitly contained in the document. The subject matter described in a claim of an application under examination is thus compared element by element with the contents of each individual publication. Lack of novelty can only be found if the publication by itself contains all the characteristics of that claim, that is, if it anticipates the subject matter of the claim.

Obviousness

Lack of novelty may however, be implicit in the publication in the sense that, in carrying out the "teaching" of the publication, a person having ordinary skill in the art would inevitably arrive at a result falling within the terms of the claim. Generally speaking, lack of novelty of this kind is termed as "obvious". That is it should not be obvious to lay man or the person skilled in art. Which means the invention should not be the product of common sense of a lay man or person qualified in the state of technology.

1.5 Inventive Step (Non-Obviousness) and Industrial Application

Inventive Step (Non-Obviousness)

The inventive step, is that technological contribution of Inventor which leads to Novelty. It should be noted that novelty and inventive step are different criteria. Novelty exists if there is any difference between the invention and the prior art. The question, "is there inventive step?" only arises if there is novelty. The expression "inventive step" conveys the idea that it is not enough that the claimed invention is new, that is, different from what exists in the state of the art, but that this difference must have two characteristics. Firstly, it must be "inventive", that is, the result of a creative idea, and it must be a step, that is, it must be noticeable. There must be a clearly identifiable difference between the state of the art and the claimed invention. This is why, in some jurisdictions, there is the concept of an "advance" or "progress" over the prior art. Secondly, it is required that this advance or progress be **significant and essential to the invention.** In order to establish inventive step, prior art as a whole has to be considered. In assessment of novelty, the subject matter of the claim in patent application is compared not with each publication or other disclosure separately, but with the combinations thereof, insofar as each such combination is obvious to the person having ordinary skill in the art. The combination may be global, whereas the claim may define a set of subject matter known separately, for instance a new form of washing machine including a particular type of motor coupled to a particular type of pump. **For the inventive step to be denied, it is necessary that not only the combination, but also the choice of the combined elements, is obvious. It is the sum of the differences that have been discovered which must be compared with the prior art and judged as to obviousness, and not each of the new elements taken individually, except where there is no technical link between them.** In most cases, it is useful to assess inventive step in relation to three aspects, namely:

- the problem to be solved;
- the solution to that problem; and
- the advantageous effects, if any, of the invention with reference to the background art. If the problem is known or obvious, the examination will bear on the originality of the solution claimed. If no inventive step is found in the solution, the question becomes whether or not the

result is obvious or whether it is surprising either by its nature or by its extent. If a person having ordinary skill in the art would have been able to pose the problem, solve it in the manner claimed, and foresee the result, the inventive step is lacking. Considering the question what is an 'invention', it was held in *Raj Parkash v. Mangat Ram Choudhary,* that "invention is to find out or discover something not found or discovered by anyone before and not necessarily the invention should be complicated and the requirement is that the inventor was the first one to adopt it and the principle therefore is that every simple invention that is claimed, so long as it is something novel or new, would be an invention and the claims and the specifications have to be understand in that light and a new invention may consist of a new combination of all integers so as to produce a new or important result or may consist of altogether new integers and the claims for anticipation by the defendant has to be either by prior user or by prior publication". It was further observed that "whether a patent sets out an invention is to be determined by a true and fair construction of the specifications and the claims and in construing the specifications it would be erroneous to rely too much on the title thereof because the title cannot control the actual claim and a misleading title similarly is of no consequence and the words of the specifications should be given their ordinary meaning but where necessary must be construed in the sense in which they are used in a particular trade or sphere in which the invention is sought to have been made and it is the pith and marrow of the invention that has to be looked into and one should not get bogged down or involved in the detailed specifications and claims made by the parties who claim to be patentee or alleged violators". Hence ***"inventive step" means a feature of an invention that involves technical advance as compared to the existing knowledge or having economic significance or both and that makes the invention not obvious to a person skilled in the art.***

Inventions Not Patentable

Mere discovery of any new use of known substance

A mere discovery of new property of known substance is not considered patentable. **For instance**:1. new use of Aspirin for treatment of the cardiovascular disease, which was earlier used for analgesic purpose, is not patentable. However, a new and alternative process for preparing Aspirin is patentable. Similarly the new use of methyl alcohol as antifreeze in automobiles. The use of methanol as a solvent is known in the prior art. A new use has been claimed in this claim as antifreeze which is not allowable. Further, a new use of Chloroquine for Sarcoidosis (a fungal disease) and for Infectious mononucleosis (a viral disease) and for Diabetic neuritis (inflammation of nerves) is not patentable. The mere use of a known process, machine or apparatus unless such known process results in a new product or employs at least one new reactant:- Mere use of a known process is **not patentable** unless such known process results in a new product or employs at least one new reactant. **2**. mere use of known apparatus or machine for another purpose is also not considered patentable. In one application there was a claim relating to a food-packing machine used for packing the desired amount of talcum powder, since it did not characterize any changes in the food-packing machine, it was presumed that the same machine had been used for the purpose of packing talcum powder. Therefore, it was understood from the claim that the same packing machine, which was in vogue, was used for packing the material other than food. Hence this was not allowed. **3**. a mixture of sugar and some colourants in water to produce a soft drink is a mere admixture resulting into aggregation of the properties. Similarly, a mixture of different types of medicament or medicine to cure multiple diseases is also a mere admixture of substances and is not a patentable invention.

While in one application which was for the invention "Apparatus for the utilization of high-pressure steam produced in a pressure vessel particularly in a domestic pressure cooker. One of the grounds of **opposition** was that the coffee attachment "esteem" sold by M/s. S. Mangal Singh & Co., Meerut prior to 16th December,1975 i.e. filing date had most of the features of the invention and, therefore the invention was in prior use. The Controller obtained that the applicants invention comprised in combination (i) a domestic pressure cooker having an additional vent provided and located on the lid of the said cooker; (ii) said vent having a screw threaded or slotted outlet in seal-tight engagement with said vent; (iii) control means for controlling the supply of high pressure steam; (iv) a conduit pipe; (v) one end of said conduit pipe being in connected in seal tight engagement with said screw threaded or slotted outlet for conveying the high pressure steam and supply means connected to the other end of said conduit pipe. He further observed that the coffee attachment Esteem' was press fitted on the hole or vent in the centre of the lid of a pressure cooker by removing the weight valve and its supporting unit whereas in applicant's invention additional vent was provided in the lid and the whole construction of the applicant's apparatus was different. In the "Esteeem' the weight valve was fitted on the top of the attachment to build up the pressure in the pressure cooker whereas in the applicant's invention weight valve remains at its own place. Accordingly it was concluded that the coffee attachment "Esteem' sold by M/s. S. Mangal Singh & Co., Meeut prior to the 16th December, 1975 was not the same as claimed by the applicant in his complete specification. Therefore, the question of prior use of applicant's invention does not arise.

No patent shall be granted for the invention which in the opinion of Central Government is useful for or related to the production, control, use or disposal of atomic energy or prospecting mining extraction, production, physical and chemical treatment fabrication, enrichment, canning or use of any prescribed substance or radioactive substance or the insuring of safety in atomic energy operation. According to Section 20(1) of Atomic Energy Act, atomic energy means energy released from atomic nuclei as a result of any process including the fission and fusion processes. Under this Act, "prescribed substances" means any substance including any mineral which the Central Government may, by notification, prescribe, being a substance which in its opinion is or may be used for the production or use of atomic energy or research into matters connected therewith and includes uranium, plutonium, thorium, beryllium, deuterium or any of these respective derivative or compounds or any other materials containing any of the aforesaid substances. The Act defines the term "radioactive substances" or "radioactive material" as any substance or material, which spontaneously emits radiation in excess of the levels prescribed by notification by the Central Government.

The section 4.1 of Indian Patent Act deals with "Inventions - non-patentable" describes certain products and processes, which are not to be regarded as patentable inventions as per the Act. Section 3a) Some examples of a frivolous nature and contrary to natural laws are:-

a. A machine purporting to produce perpetual motion.

b. A machine alleged to be giving output without any input.

c. "A method of showing time on the basis of metric system" wherein dial of time piece having three hands for indicating, hour, minutes and seconds was divided into 10 parts for hours, each hour into 100 minutes and each minute into 100 seconds. The invention was held frivolous and not considered a patentable invention. (Indian patent application No. 101/Bom/72).

d. Merely making in one piece, articles previously made in two or more pieces is frivolous. Mere usefulness is not sufficient [*Indian Vacuum Brake' Company Ltd v. Laurd* (AIR 1962, Cal 152)].

e. A machine allegedly giving 100% performance.

3(b) "An invention the primary or intended use or commercial exploitation of which could be contrary public order or morality or which causes serious prejudice to human, animal or plant life or health or to the environment."

Some examples are:

(i) An invention, the use of which is contrary to the law which is in force, or use of which is prohibited such as,

   a. Any device, apparatus or machine or method for committing theft/burglary,

b. Any machine or method for counterfeiting of currency notes,

c. Any device or method for gambling,

d. An invention the use of which can cause injury to human beings, plants and animals.

(ii) Inventions, the established or intended use or commercial exploitation of which is found to be injurious to public, animal or plant life or health, such as, a method of adulteration of food.

(iii) An invention, the present or intended use of which is likely to violate the well accepted and settled social, cultural, legal norms of morality, e.g. method of cloning

(iv) An invention, the primary or proposed use of which would disturb the public orders e.g. a device for house-breaking.

(v) Terminator gene technology

3(c) "The mere discovery of a scientific principle or the formulation of an abstract theory or discovery of any living thing or non-living substances occurring in nature"

There is a difference between discovery and invention. A discovery adds to the amount of human knowledge by disclosing something already existent, which has not been seen before, whereas an invention adds to the human knowledge by creating a new product or processes involving a technical advance as compared to the existing knowledge. A claim for discovery of scientific principle is not considered patentable, but such a principle when used with process of manufacture resulting into a substance or an article may be patentable. A scientific theory is a statement about the natural world. These theories themselves are not considered patentable, no matter how radical or revolutionary an insight they may provide, since they do not result in a product or process. However, if the theories lead to practical application in the process of manufacture of article or substance, they may well be patentable. A claim for formulation of abstract theory is not patentable. For example, the fact that a known material or article is found to have a hitherto unknown property is a discovery and not an invention. **But if the discovery leads to the conclusion that the material can be used for making a particular article or in a particular process, then the article or process could be patentable.** Finding out that a particular known material is able to withstand mechanical shock is a discovery and therefore not patentable, but a claim to a railway sleeper made of the material would not fall foul of this exclusion, and would be allowable if it passed the tests for novelty and inventive step. Similarly, finding of a new substance or micro-organism occurring freely in nature is a discovery and not an invention e.g. in *Kirin-Amgen v. Hoechst Marion Roussel* [2005] RPC 9].

3(d) *The mere discovery of a new form of a known substance which does not result in the enhancement of the known efficacy of that substance or the mere discovery of any new property or new use for a known substance or of the mere use of a known process, machine or apparatus unless such known process results in a new product or employs at least one new reactant.*

For example salts, esters, ethers, polymorphs, metabolites, pure form, particle size, isomers, mixtures of isomers, complexes, combinations and other derivatives of known substance shall be considered to be the same substance, unless they differ significantly in properties with regard to efficacy. A mere discovery of new property of known substance is not considered patentable. For instance, new use of Aspirin for treatment of the cardiovascular disease, which was earlier used for analgesic purpose, is not patentable. However, a new and alternative process for preparing Aspirin is patentable. The mere use of a known process, machine or apparatus unless such known process results in a new product or employs at least one new reactant; Mere use of a known process is not patentable unless such known process results in a new product or employs at least one new reactant. Similarly mere use of known apparatus or machine for another purpose is also not considered patentable. A mere juxtaposition of features, already known before the priority date, which have been chosen arbitrarily from amongst a number of a different combinations, which could be chosen, is not a patentable invention.

Industrial Application

Industrial application is another essential criterion for patentability. An invention, must be of a kind which can be applied for practical purposes, not be purely theoretical. If the invention is intended to be a product or part of a product, it should be possible to make that product. And if the invention is intended to be a process or part of a process, it should be possible to carry that process out or "use" it (the general term) in practice. "Applicability" and "industrial applicability" are expressions reflecting, respectively, the possibility of making and manufacturing in practice, and that of carrying out or using in practice. The term "industrial" should be considered in its broadest sense, including any kind of industry. In common language, an "industrial" activity means a technical activity on a certain scale, and the "industrial" applicability of an invention means the application (making use) of an invention by technical means on a certain scale. National and regional laws and practices concerning the industrial applicability requirement vary significantly. At one end of the spectrum, the requirement of industrial applicability is met as long as the claimed invention can be made in industry without taking into account the use of the invention. Precisely, the "usefulness" of the claimed invention is taken into account for the determination of the industrial applicability. On the other hand, some countries do not require industrial applicability, but utility.

Chapter - 2

Patent Specification Drafting

2.1 Specification Drafting

The first task in drafting a patent application is the identification of the invention. This involves a) summarizing all the necessary features which in combination solve a particular technical problem; and b) an examination of this combination to determine whether it would, according to one's own judgment, fulfill the requirements for patentability, **especially inventive step**. It is during this process that a full comprehension of the essence of the invention is obtained, and this is important in helping to draft the description and claims.

Often the invention contains more than one new feature. It is essential to identify the critical feature or features and to have an explanation of why they contribute to an effective solution to the problem. There are two important reasons for this. First, the claims should be as broad as possible; the broadest claim is the one restricted by the least number of features. Second, having identified the critical features and their effect, it is then necessary to ask how else may this effect be achieved, that is, can the specific features be substituted or altered while still achieving the end result. This is important not only in drafting the claims, which must be wide enough to cover these substitutes or alternatives, but also in the description of the invention which must include details of the substitutes or alternatives so that the broad claim can be supported by the description. Once invention is ascertained google test should be done for Novelty. After clearing that test you need to check at various technical websites like pubmed in biosciences. After you yourself become sure about the novelty of your invention you have two options: Filing for search before filing patent application (application is also termed as specification) to the patent office or simply filing patent application to patent office along with prescribed form and fee. It all depends on your strategy. Now before filing you need to decide that whether you should file provisional specification or complete specification. The difference between the two is: Provisional application gives you the protection of date and twelve months of time period to validate your invention which further helps the inventor in drafting claims.

The provisional application goes without claims while claims have to be incorporated in complete specification in India.

2.2 Method and Precautions in Drafting Patent Specification

Three basic requirements, to be complied with in the drafting of a patent application. Firstly, there is a requirement that the application should relate to **one invention only**, or to a group of inventions so linked as to form a single general inventive concept. This requirement, referred to as "unity of invention", is particularly important when claims are being drafted. Secondly, the description should disclose the invention in a manner sufficiently clear and complete for the invention to be evaluated, and to be carried out by a person having ordinary skill in the art. This is of fundamental importance, since one of the main functions of the description is to provide new technical information to third parties. An important phrase to note in this requirement is "a person having ordinary skill in the art." This allows for a simplified description since it can be assumed that the reader will be an informed reader having the background knowledge which makes it unnecessary to describe every basic detail of the invention. Thirdly, for the application to proceed, it must contain claims which determine the scope of the protection. The claims must be clear and concise and fully supported by the description. This third basic requirement is important since the claims are the basis of interpretation of patent protection. It is from the claims that third parties are able to know what they may do and what they may not do. The claims may not be significantly broader or different from that which has been described.

The first section of the description typically contains two elements, first, the **title of the invention** with address and a brief statement of the technical field in which the invention lies. Usually this statement is in the form of a short introductory paragraph which commences with the phrase "This invention relates to ......". Second element is, the background of the invention also termed as **prior art**. In drafting this section, all the existing knowledge in the subject matter relevant to signify invention should be mentioned. Existing problems or difficulties which the invention overcomes or any previous solutions to those problems or difficulties should be described, preferably in a way which clearly sets out the difference between the present and previous solutions. The second section of the description is the **object of the invention**, that is to say, what the invention sets out to achieve. This section of the description is important to provide a good understanding of the invention and to put it into perspective against the prior art. The third section of the description provides a **summary of the invention** in such terms that it may be readily understood. The patent agent will normally describe the invention first in general terms which correspond to those he intends to use in the main claim. By using this technique, the agent can avoid any disputes that might arise based on differences between the invention described and the invention as defined in the claims. This description of the invention in general terms is usually followed by a series of paragraphs which set out different preferred features of the invention. These paragraphs usually form the basis for dependent claims which follow the broad main claim. In the fourth section of the description, two elements are generally found, namely a brief description of the drawings, if drawings are appropriate, and a detailed description of one or more embodiments of the invention. If the invention relates to some form of mechanical object, for example, drawings illustrating plan, elevation and sectional views of that object could be used. Elements of the drawings which are described are numbered in the drawings and these numbers utilized in the description of the embodiment. Where the invention is an electrical circuit, drawings can be used effectively to show the connections between the various elements or components of the circuit. Again these elements or components should be numbered for ease of reference. Normally the drawings should contain no textual matter. Exceptions, however, may be made when single descriptive words can be used where they do not interfere with the lines of the drawings. Thus in any drawing illustrating an electrical circuit, for example, standard components may be indicated in the drawings by boxes which may be labelled. Similarly, where the invention relates to a process, drawings may show a block, schematic or flow-sheet diagram, and blocks or boxes contained therein may be labelled as appropriate. Where the invention is in the chemical field, the drawing may be the chemical formula of one or more compounds. Where the invention is of a metallurgical nature, the drawing may be a diagram such as a phase diagram of the components. It is usual for the description of the embodiment to include a passage which briefly describes the actual operation of the invention. If the device, for example, is a machine or an electrical circuit, the manner in which the machine or electrical circuit operates is extremely helpful in understanding the invention. Description is followed by claims. Claims should be drafted on fresh page starting with I claim or we claim.

The last element of a patent is the abstract. The abstract presents a short summary of the description and the claims. It serves the purpose of enabling third parties to obtain quick information about the essential contents of the invention. It must be emphasized that it is not used to interpret the scope of protection. The abstract should be so drafted that it can efficiently serve as a scanning tool for purposes of searching in the particular art. Thus the abstract has to be as concise as the disclosure permits. Generally speaking, it contains between 50 and 150 words.

Title : The title should give a fair indication of the art or industry to which the invention relates. It should be brief, free from fancy expressions, free from ambiguity and as precise and definite as possible but it need not go into the details of the invention itself and should be normally within 15 words. It should verbally agree with the title stated in application. The followings are not allowable in the title: Inventor's name; the word 'Patent'; words in other languages; the abbreviation "etc"; fancy words, e.g., "Washwell Soap", "Universal Rest Easy Patent Chair".

2.3 Disclosure Requirements

An additional requirement of patentability is whether or not the invention is sufficiently disclosed in the application. The application must disclose the invention in a manner sufficiently clear for the invention to be carried out by a person skilled in the art. The description should set out at least one mode for carrying out the invention claimed. This should be done in terms of examples, where appropriate, and with reference to the drawings, if any. The description is required to disclose the best mode for carrying out the invention known to the applicant. There are two basic requirements of disclosure, first oppositions may be filed, the public must be informed of the content of the application, and this is done by the Patent Office by publication of a notice in an official journal or gazette. After this publication the application is open to public inspection; second, the disclosure in detail description makes the basis of claims. The subject matter written in claims must be disclosed in the description section otherwise claims are rejected by the examiner. Any application can be opposed on the grounds of novelty, inventive step or industrial applicability, insufficient disclosure of the invention, or the fact that an amendment made to a patent application has gone beyond the original disclosure in the application as filed.

2.4 Patent Claims

The claims are the centre or the heart of any granted patent because the rights are granted on the claims. They define the protection which is the purpose of the patent, that is to say, they define clearly the scope of the exclusive right provided by the patent. Therefore it is the most important task in preparing the application, to produce a wording of the claims which defines the invention in terms of the technical features disclosed in the description and which does not contain any reference to commercial advantages. Claims are always drafted on separate page and claim one is the **main claim** which should be single sentence and broad. This first claim followed by a number of claims of narrower scope. The broad claim is drafted so as to just avoid the prior art known at the time of preparing the application. The succeeding claims is drafted more narrowly, and hopefully this results in stronger claims which could withstand any anticipation by more relevant prior art which might be produced by a Patent Office during examination, or by third parties during any opposition or invalidation proceeding. It should be noted that there must be some element of additional invention in each succeeding claim in order for it to be stronger. The narrower claims following the broad main claim usually refer back to one or more of the preceding claims. They are therefore usually called **dependent claims**. The features introduced in each of the dependent claims must find some basis in the description. There it is usually explained that these are preferred features which produce a better technical form of the invention.

The claims relating to software programme product are computer programme simply expressed on a computer readable storage medium and as such are not allowable. For example, if the new feature comprises a set of instructions (programme) designed to control a known computer to cause it to perform desired operations, without special adoption or modification of its hardware or organization, then no matter whether claimed as "a computer arranged to operate" or as "a method of operating a computer", is not patentable and hence excluded from patentability. The claim might stipulate that the instructions were encoded in a particular way on a particular known medium but this would not affect the issue. e.g., A program to evaluate the value of PI or to find the square root of a number are held not allowable. An invention consisting of hardware along with software or computer program in order to perform the function of the hardware may be considered patentable. *e.g.* embedded systems.

2.5 Filing of A Patent Application

Persons entitled to file patent application:

(a) Any person claiming to be the true and first inventor of the invention;

(b) any person being the assignee of the person claiming to be the true and first inventor in respect of the right to make such an application;

(c) the legal representative of any deceased person who immediately before his death was entitled to make such an application.

The term "person" includes any company or association or body of individual, whether incorporated or not in the case of a limited partnership, the application may be in the names of all personally responsible partners.

The patent application can be filed at the head office of the patent office or the branch office, as the case may be, within whose territorial limits—

(a) the applicant or first mentioned applicant in case of joint applicants for a patent, normally resides or has his domicile or has a place of business or the place from where the invention actually originated; or (b) the applicant for a patent or party in a proceeding if he has no place of business or domicile in India, the address for service in India given by such applicant or party is situated; and the appropriate office once decided in respect of any proceedings under the Act shall not ordinarily be changed.

There are four Patent Offices in India. Their place of location and territorial jurisdictions are: **Mumbai Patent Office:** The States of Gujarat, Maharashtra, Madhya Pradesh, Goa, Chhattisgarh, the Union Territories of Daman & Diu and Dadra & Nagar Haveli.

Delhi Patent Office: : The States of Haryana, Himachal Pradesh, Jammu and Kashmir, Punjab, Rajasthan, Uttar Pradesh, Uttaranchal, National Capital Territory of Delhi and the Union Territory of Chandigarh.

Chennai Patent Office: The States of Andhra Pradesh, Karnataka, Kerala, Tamil Nadu and the Union Territories of Pondecherry and Lakshdweep.

Kolkata Patent Office: Rest of India.

International application under the Patent Cooperation Treaty for a patent, as may be filed designating India shall be deemed to be an application under this Act, if a corresponding application has also been filed before the Controller in India. The filing date of an international application and complete specification processed by the Indian patent office shall be the international filing date accorded under the Patent Cooperation Treaty.

Where the application is made by virtue of an assignment of the right to apply for a patent for the invention, there shall be furnished with the application, or within such period as may be prescribed after the filing of the application, proof of the right to make the application. Every application shall state that the applicant is in possession of the invention and shall name the person claiming to be the true and first inventor; and where the person so claiming is not the applicant or one of the applicants, the application shall contain a declaration on prescribed form that the applicant believes the person so named to be the true and first inventor. All documents and copies of documents, except affidavits and drawings should be submitted to patent office in the name of Controller of patents, shall be written or typewritten or printed either in Hindi or in English language in large and legible characters with deep indelible ink with lines widely spaced upon one side only of strong white paper of a size A4 of approximately 29.7 centimetres by 21 centimetres with a margin of at least 4 centimetres on the top and left hand part and 3cm on the bottom and right hand part thereof. Any signature which is not legible or which is written in a script other than Hindi or English shall be accompanied by a transcription of the name either in Hindi or in English in block letters.

Chapter - 3

IPR Issues

3.1 Comparative and Collaborative Research

The research is done involving many experts from different fields of knowledge. This compels one to collaborate with other institutes. The moment collaboration is thought various Intellectual Property (IP) related issues originates and the research becomes very competitive. There is a mode of handling such complexities by signing agreements between the collaborating institutions. First of all each party's confidential information has to be protected. This knowledge is the background disclosed by one party to the other for use in the project.

In collaborative research agreement is done between the partners in such a way that which does not affect the IP of either party in any area of technology, design, work, invention, software, data, technique, know how or materials. The Intellectual Property Rights (IPR) remains the property of the party which contributes to project. Where any third party such as a student or contractor is involved in the project, the institute or the party engaging that contractor (as the case may be) will ensure that the student and the contractor assigns any Intellectual Property Rights which they may acquire I the duration of the project. The rights of either partner in collaborative research is protected through signing of Non Disclosure Agreements and Confidential Agreements (NDA

& CDA) to enable them discuss work undertaken as part of the project in Institute seminars, tutorials and lectures. It is important to the career prospects of many academic researchers that they may publish articles and participate in conferences. Therefore the University and its academics will nearly always wish to publish information about the project. If the project is sponsored, the Institute shall submit to the sponsor, in writing, details of any results which any employee or student of the Institute intends to publish, at least 60 days before the date of proposed submission for publication. In competitive research it is likely that each party will make available for use in the Project, information, software or materials which already exist or which are developed independently of project. The agreement shall come between the collaborators to allow its background to be used for the purposes of the project but not for any other purpose. Although it may not be possible to identify all of the background at the start of the project, if the success of the project depends on one or both of the parties making certain background available, this needs to be identified and described in the agreement. Unless identified background is included in agreement as one of the items that a party in collaboration is obliged to provide that party is not obliged to provide any background. That will not prevent it providing background if it wishes to do so. If any of the background is sensitive or for some other reason should not be disclosed beyond the researchers working on the project, this should be identified either before, or at the when the background is made available. While academic researchers may want to publish as part of their academic publication of the results, it may be important that background of the other party remains confidential. It is important that this issue is resolved at the outset. The university may favours the joint ownership of the Intellectual Property Rights (IPR) in the results and the parties may welcome them as an 'easy solution', in that case both the parties will be joint owners. Under the Indian Patent Law:

- if the patent is granted to two or more persons each of them has equal rights in the invention unless they agree to the contrary; if there are three patent owners, each will have a one-third right in the patent unless they have entered into agreement which determines other shares in the invention and in the revenues from it.

- each patent owner may work his share for his own benefit without accounting to the other owner(s) but
- a license of the patent may not be granted without the permission of the other owners. The Controller may, on application, intervene if this is flouted.

In collaborative research thoughts need to be given to:

a) Co-operation in filing for any patent or registering any other IPR which is jointly owned.

b) Both of the joint owners joining in anyaction against infringers

c) Sharing of revenues.

3.2 The Strategy to Protecting Plants: Plant Variety Protection Act

According to Section 3(j) of the Indian Patent Act plants and animals as whole or any part thereof other than micro-organisms but including seeds, varieties and species and essentially biological processes for production or propagation of plants and animals are not patentable inventions.

The availability to growers of improved, new plant varieties is critically important to the agricultural and horticultural industries of all countries. Improved disease resistance, higher yields and improvements in a host of other features of plants can dramatically affect the economics of the production of a crop and its acceptability to its final consumers. Food security for a rapidly growing world population, sustainable agricultural production, the need to raise farm incomes and to enhance economic development call for sustained efforts in breeding new varieties. However, new varieties, developed after many years of patient work and heavy investment, are frequently capable of self-reproduction, with the result that the release of a small quantity of reproductive material of a plant variety can mean that it is thenceforth available to all. Since the plant breeder is unable to secure a sufficient economic return from the initial release of material of his variety, the granting to breeders of rights of exclusive exploitation of their varieties has proved to be essential to provide an incentive for private investment in plant breeding in many species.

As early as 1930, the United States of America introduced a special form of exclusive right called a plant patent, which was, however, available only for asexually reproduced varieties. Subsequently a group of European States came together in 1961 to establish the International Convention for the Protection of New Varieties of Plants (the Convention), which was revised in 1972, 1978 and 1991. The Convention also establishes the International Union for the Protection of New Varieties of Plants which is known as UPOV (the name "UPOV" is an acronym derived from the French translation of these words); its 1978 revised form is hereafter referred to as "the 1978 Act." The Convention as revised in 1991 is called "the 1991 Act." The Convention potentially protects all plant varieties irrespective of their mode of reproduction or of the technology used in their development. States adhering to the Convention undertake to create a system for the grant of plant breeders' rights, within their domestic laws, in accordance with internationally agreed and uniform principles. Each UPOV Member State must entrust the granting of breeders' rights to an appropriate administrative unit. Plant breeders' rights are granted in each Member State for its own territory, and not on an international basis. After the entry into force of the 1991 Act, on April 24, 1998, the 1978 Act was closed for further accessions with the exception of those States which had already initiated the accession procedure by that time. UPOV is an independent, international, intergovernmental organization, with an international legal personality. Its headquarters are in Geneva, and it employs its own staff. UPOV cooperates very closely in administrative matters with the World Intellectual Property Organization (WIPO), a specialized agency of the United Nations. The Secretary-General of UPOV is the Director General of WIPO, the UPOV headquarters is in the same building as WIPO, and UPOV receives a range of support services from WIPO. Existing member States only become bound by the 1991 Act when they have modified their existing laws and deposited an instrument of accession to the new Act. The 1978 Act provides a system for the protection of a new plant variety, that is to say, the physical unit of plant material selected by the plant breeder with its set of morphological and physiological characteristics. If a legal right in this unit of plant material is to be effectively enforced, the identity of the plant material must be established beyond doubt. When concluding whether particular plant material constitutes or belongs to a "variety", the classifier must decide on the extent of its distinctness from other material, its uniformity in the sense that variations from a standard description are within reasonable limits and its stability in the sense that it will retain its distinguishing features from one generation to the next. The 1978 Act accordingly requires that member States adopt the three criteria of distinctness, uniformity and stability as the technical basis for the protection of plant varieties, and adds the further two requirements of commercial novelty and the submission of an acceptable denomination for the variety. A variety must be commercially novel to secure protection and that the variety must not, prior to the date of application, have been offered for sale or marketed with the agreement of the breeder in the territory of the State where the application in question has been filed. States are, however, given a choice in relation to this provision and are permitted, if they wish, to permit varieties to be offered for sale or market in their own territories for a maximum of one year prior to the date of application. In addition, the variety must not have been offered for sale or marketed with the agreement of the breeder in the territory of any other state for longer than six years, in the case of certain woody species, or for four years in the case of all other species. These periods of grace relating to commercialization in other countries recognize the lengthy nature of trials to ascertain the agronomic value of varieties before making an application for protection, without prejudicing the right to protection. The technical criteria of **distinctness, uniformity and stability, commercial novelty** and the establishment of a denomination accordingly represent the standard conditions that must be fulfilled to secure protection for a new plant variety under the laws of UPOV Member States. The Act establishes the nature of the rights that member States must as a minimum undertake to grant to breeders. The breeder's right is limited to the exclusive production and sale of reproductive or vegetative propagating material of his variety. The breeder does not, for instance, in the case of a cereal variety, have the exclusive right to sell grain of that variety, but only seed. It is a question of fact to be established by evidence whether a sale is of seed or grain. A further very important aspect to note here is that under the 1978 Act the breeder's exclusive right relates only to production for the purposes of commercial marketing. If production of reproductive material is not for that purpose, or if such material is not marketed, it is not covered by the breeders' rights: a farmer, for instance, who produces seed on his own farm for the purposes of re-sowing on his own farm, can do so freely without obligation to the breeder. The 1978 Act only establishes the minimum scope of the right that States must grant. The Act further provides that any authorization given by the breeder in relation to the production or marketing of his variety may be made subject to such conditions as he may specify. The breeder is thus to be free to decide whether he will exploit his exclusive right by producing and selling all the reproductive or propagating material of his variety that is needed by the market, or whether he will grant licenses to others, perhaps in exchange for a royalty. The breeder is content to receive a royalty on each ton of seed which is sold. In the case of more specialized seed production such as the production of some cross-pollinating species, of hybrid varieties, of high-quality vegetable seed or of new varieties of trees or vines, the practice of the breeder is probably to control very tightly the production of seed or plants in order to maintain the quality and reputation of his variety. In these cases he may seek his reward directly in the price of the seed. Many different situations exist, however, depending upon the commercial structure of seed and nursery plant distribution and the logistical aspects of the production and distribution of a particular species. The 1978 Act is silent on all these marketing questions. It simply requires of UPOV member States that they permit breeders to specify conditions of licenses for their varieties. It states that the authorization of the breeder shall not be required for the utilization of the variety as an initial source of variation for the purpose of creating other varieties. The only permitted exception to this rule arises when the repeated use of the variety is necessary for the commercial production of another variety. This limited exception relates to the use of an inbred line in the commercial production of seed of a hybrid. The free availability of protected varieties as a germ plasm source for other breeders is a fundamental tenet of the 1978 Act, and demonstrates that its authors were agriculturalists who were totally aware of the nature of plant breeding and of the manner in which incremental progress is achieved by building upon the progress embodied in existing varieties. It requires States to grant a minimum period of protection of 18 years in the case of vines, forest trees, fruit trees, and ornamental trees and 15 years in the case of all other plants. The Act does not immediately impose upon its member States the obligation to protect all botanical genera and species. The 1978 Act states that its provisions *may be applied* to all botanical genera and species, without requiring member States to protect all these. What it does require is that Member States apply the Convention to a minimum of five genera when first acceding to the UPOV Convention and that, over a period of years, they progressively apply the Convention to a greater number of protected species. Most Member States protect all species of economic importance in their countries and, in an increasing number of cases, the entire plant kingdom. It also includes that the breeder of a protected variety shall forfeit his right if he is no longer in a position to provide the authorities with reproductive or propagating material capable of reproducing the protected variety, with its morphological and physiological characteristics, as defined when the right was granted. In other words, the breeder must competently maintain his variety if he wishes to retain the benefit of protection. The Act provides that a state may provide protection for plant varieties in the form of plant variety protection or of a patent, but once it has opted to protect varieties of a species by plant breeders' rights it may not subsequently protect varieties of that same specie by patent. This is the so-called prohibition on "double protection." The Act provides that UPOV member States may not restrict the exercise of the exclusive right accorded to the breeder otherwise than for reasons of public interest and that, where any such restriction is imposed, the Member State involved shall take all necessary measures to ensure that the breeder receives equitable remuneration. It provides that the right of the breeder should not be annulled unless it is shown that the variety did not fulfil the commercial novelty and distinctness requirements when the rights were granted, or be cancelled unless the breeder fails to maintain the variety or pay the necessary fees. The Act requires member States to establish rules giving priority for a period of 12 months to an application for a variety where an application has already been filed for that variety in another country. This means that an application in a Member State must be treated as if filed on the date of an earlier application in another member State for which priority is claimed. The grant or refusal of breeders' rights for a variety must be independent of the regulation in any UPOV Member State which is concerned with the production, certification and marketing of seeds.

3.3 IPR Issues in Biotechnological Patents Haldi, Neem and Basmati Rice

Infringement is a smart mode of bio-piracy. Knowingly or unknowingly people file the patent on obvious subject matter and patent is sometimes granted also. Oppositions are the way to get over with such mistakes. Some good examples are the case of granted patent of USPTO (United States Patent and Trademark Office) on wound healing properties of Turmeric Powder. This was opposed by Govt. of India on the basis of traditional knowledge known to the country from generations and causing revoke of the patent. In 1995 two Indian scientists working at an American University received a US patent for a method of using turmeric to treat wounds after complete validation of the property on animal models. Their claims were challenged by the Indian Council of Scientific and Industrial Research in March 1995. In fact this case is very good example of **"knowledge known in any form"** and overcoming the Novelty. Commonly Turmeric, and Neem case studies are presented as the bio-piracy cases. But in my opinion it is the incompetency of examining authority which grants the patent on known things. In my opinion **this was neither infringement nor bio-piracy as there was no violation of any**

IPR. Similarly one of the patent obtained by WR Grace & Co for stabilizing *azadirachtin*. The USPTO granted another patent to the US Company WR Grace on a process to extract and stabilize an *azadirachtin*-based (*aza-A*) pesticide from Neem seed. The US Environmental Protection Agency (EPA) first approved *aza-A* for use on the US market in 1985. In 1988, Robert Larson, a US timber importer who received this approval sold the patent on an extraction process to the US company WR Grace. Four years later, WR Grace began to market the insecticide under the name *Margosan O* for use on non-food crops. The patent has been granted on an extraction and solving process that makes the end product more stable and therefore gives it a longer shelf life, from a few days to up to two years. This was also revoked on the basis of lack of Novelty. Another similar example is of US Patent granted for Rice. In late 1997, an American company Rice Tec Inc, was granted a patent by the US patent office to call the aromatic rice grown outside India 'Basmati'. RiceTec Inc, had been trying to enter the international Basmati market with brands like 'Kasmati' and 'Texmati' described as Basmati-type rice with minimal success. However, with the Basmati patent rights, RiceTec would be able to not only call its aromatic rice Basmati within the US, but also label it Basmati for its exports. This has grave repercussions for India and Pakistan because not only India would have lost out on the 45,000 tonne US import market, which forms 10 percent of the total Basmati exports, but also its position in crucial markets like the European Union, the United Kingdom, Middle East and West Asia. In addition, the patent on Basmati was believed to be a violation of the fundamental fact that the long grain aromatic rice grown only in Punjab, Haryana, and Uttar Pradesh was called Basmati. According to sources from the Indian Newspaper, Economic Times, "Patenting Basmati in the US was like snatching away our history and culture." The company in abstract wrote "the invention relates to novel rice lines and to plants and grains of these lines. The invention also relates to a novel means for determining the cooking and starch properties of rice grains and its use in identifying desirable rice lines. Specifically, one aspect of the invention relates to novel rice lines whose plants are semi-dwarf in stature, substantially photoperiod insensitive and high yielding, and produce rice grains having characteristics similar or superior to those of good quality Basmati rice. Another aspect of the invention relates to novel rice lines produced from novel rice lines. The invention provides a method for breeding these novel lines. A third aspect...relates to the finding that the starch index (SI) of a rice grain can predict the grain's cooking and starch properties, to a method based thereon for identifying grains that can be cooked to the firmness of traditional Basmati rice preparations, and to the use of this method in selecting desirable segregants in rice breeding programs." In an official release, the government of India reacted immediately after learning of the Basmati patent issued to RiceTec Inc., stating that it would approach the US patent office and urge them to re-examine the patent to a United States firm to grow and sell rice under the Basmati brand name in order to protect India's interests, particularly those of growers and exporters. Furthermore, a high level inter-ministerial group comprising of representatives of the ministries and departments of commerce, industry, external affairs, Council for Scientific and Industrial Research (CSIR), Agriculture, Bio-technology, All India Rice Exporters Association (AIREA), APEDA, and Indian Council of Agricultural Research (ICAR) were mobilized to begin an in-depth examination of the case. Some more related cases are: Kashmir and wood, EU-US soybean gene dispute, Chipko movement, Avocado disputes, India Tigre Trade and Tomato dispute.

3.4 Patent Litigation

In all intellectual property systems, it is common to have some form of internal appeal against a patent examiner's decision. Whatever the arrangement for internal appeal may be, in most intellectual property systems the courts play an important role in hearing appeals from decisions of the Industrial Property Office and in adjudicating infringement actions. A patent is the right enforceable in a court, usually to prevent the manufacture, sale and use of a patented invention. It is not, as many people think, permission to practice the patented invention, which may be subject to restrictions for other reasons such as security or public health. Application is made to the court to stop the unauthorized manufacture, sale or use of the invention, so that the court may grant the appropriate order and stop the infringement. In practice, however, the process is less straightforward than it sounds. When thinking about patent enforcement, a patentee must first assess what he has patented. A patent must include a specification containing claims, a description and any required drawings. The claims are decisive, as they define the scope of protection sought and eventually granted through the patent. The specification or the description and drawings may be used to interpret the claims, which must be fully supported by them. Most inventors use the services of a patent attorney to write the specification for them. An inventor may not fully understand the specification, and particularly may have difficulties in understanding the claims. Even where the patentee has some idea of the exclusive right granted to him in his own country, it is very rare for him to know with any precision what rights he may have in corresponding patents in other jurisdictions. The patentee's first real understanding of the extent of his patent rights often only comes to him when he is considering enforcement. Thus the basis for enforcement of patent rights is established at the start of the patenting process when the patent specification is written by the inventor or the inventor's patent attorney. The examination process in the Patent Office can modify the original wording. The inventor will normally try to avoid any modification which will result in a limitation of the scope of protection, for any reduction in the scope of protection makes it easier for a competitor to avoid infringement. If a competitor can easily supply the market with something that is equivalent to the invention, but does not infringe the patent, then the patent may be of limited commercial value. Patent Office examiners should try to remember this when an applicant for a patent steadfastly resists amending his claims in order to overcome an objection, but instead tries to deal with the objection by argument. While acceding to an amendment might lead to the early grant of a patent on the application, it may also lead to a patent right of doubtful commercial utility.

Evaluating Validity and Infringement of a Patent

Having assessed the scope of the patent right, the next task is for the patentee to decide if there is infringement. Before committing himself to the financial risk of a patent case — which can be among the most time-consuming and expensive of all forms of litigation — a patentee, unless he is very wealthy and relaxed about money, must make some attempt to forecast whether he can be successful. The issue of infringement is very rarely considered on its own. Patents, like other forms of intellectual property, do not only affect the parties to a dispute; they have an effect on the public at large. This being the case, it is normally considered that a patent which can be shown to be invalid cannot be enforceable. In spite of the examination of patent applications during prosecution, no patent system guarantees the validity of a granted patent. In a patent enforcement action, therefore, a defendant will usually add to any defence of non-infringement a further defence, often in the form of a counterclaim, that the patent is invalid and hence not enforceable even if infringed. In some jurisdictions, the issues of infringement and validity are heard together. In others, the question of validity is heard separately by a different court or it may be referred to the Patent Office. Because of the principle that no invalid patent should be enforceable, the defendant in a patent action is usually allowed to bring in evidence of invalidity at any stage of the proceedings, and in some jurisdictions even during the trial itself. As a result, the position of the patentee during patent enforcement proceedings tends to deteriorate as a defendant makes searches and often finds evidence which is relevant to validity. The task of the court in the determination of infringement is the assessment of the scope of protection defined by the patent and whether the alleged infringement falls within that assessed scope. In the determination of validity, the court should take the same scope of protection as has been defined for the purposes of infringement, and consider whether the evidence produced by the defendant renders the patent invalid with respect to, and to the extent of, the scope of protection claimed by the patentee. Different issues will almost always arise in these two assessments. The starting point for both, however, is almost always the wording of the claims. Frequently, there will be a problem as to whether the actual wording of the claims, if necessary interpreted in light of the specification (or the description and any drawings), defines an invention which includes the allegedly infringing subject matter.

For example, the claim may include as a feature "a spring." If the allegedly infringing device does not include a spring, but instead has a solid rubber tube which in some respects acts like a spring, can that be infringement? Different jurisdictions may handle this kind of question differently, depending on the way in which their law has developed the procedure for the definition of an invention. In addition, many courts require or expect the assistance of an expert to give guidance as to the technical merit of an argument, such as, based on the example above, that a rubber tube can be considered to fall within the term, "spring." The technical content in many patent cases can be very complex indeed, and the resolution of the technical points of dispute may not only involve one or more expert witnesses, but may need experimental evidence as well. For instance, in a case concerning the alleged infringement of a patent granted for an invention consisting of an air plasma cutting torch, the claim included a feature which defined what was happening within the torch when it was operated. To prove infringement, an experiment was necessary to define the temperature gradient of the plasma genic air within the torch itself. A probe inserted into the torch has the effect of modifying the air flow through the torch, which in turn will affect the temperature gradient. A better means of evaluation is thermal imaging, but it is expensive to set up. Assisted by arguments, which in turn are supported by expert evidence and experimental evidence, the court will reach a conclusion about whether or not an infringement has occurred. But most patents contain more than one claim. The inclusion of a number of claims is to give the patentee extra chances of preventing an infringement. If one claim is held invalid, the patentee may still succeed in restraining infringement if it is held that another claim is valid and an infringement has occurred with respect thereto. Where the patent in suit has a number of claims with respect to which the patentee alleges an infringement, the court will have to consider each claim separately to see if it is infringed.

The Cost of Patent Litigation

Whether the submission and evidence concerning infringement and validity are made in writing or given orally at a hearing, or a combination of both, the parties to a patent dispute will find themselves involved in lengthy consideration of the issues and preparation of material for the court. It is mainly the borderline cases that go to trial. This has the effect of extending the arguments by which each side hopes to secure a decision in its favour. Where the patent dispute occurs in a field of high commercial value, and most disputes are because of their high cost, the parties may be inclined to drag any point into the dispute, however peripheral, if it appears to help their case. The costs arising from all of this can become outrageous. This is really the key point about patent enforcement. However carefully one makes an estimate of the costs at the start of the litigation, they almost invariably have to be revised upwards as new issues come to light during the development of the case. Patent enforcement, or defence against enforcement, occurs because someone wishes to receive a commercial advantage, in other words, to make money. That advantage must constantly be reviewed against the cost of the litigation.

Chapter - 4

Patent Applications

4.1 Provisional and Complete Specifications

A provisional specification is not a rough draft or a skeleton of the complete specification. The complete specification, which follows a provisional specification, does not replace the latter. Both are permanent and separate documents. Provisional document is filed to get extended time period for validation of invention and protection the priority date. Main features of the provisional specification are: (a) A provisional specification should essentially contain the title and description of the invention and shall start with a preamble 'The following specification describes the invention.' Claims should not be included in the provisional specification, since it is not the purpose of Provisional Specification to claim legal right, but, to obtain priority of invention. (b) The description should start from the second page starting with the field of invention and containing the background of the invention, object of the invention, statement of the principle underlying the invention and general statement of the actual invention. It is advisable to include in the provisional specification as much information as the applicant has at the time of filing, but in any case the description should be adequate to identify the invention from the prior art. (c) It should be noted that, the provisional specification cannot be filed if the application is a divisional or convention application or an application filed under the Patent Cooperation Treaty designating India. In such cases, only a complete specification is required to be filed. (d) When an application for a patent is accompanied by a provisional specification, the complete specification (in Form 2) must be filed within **twelve months** from the date of filing of provisional specification, failing which the said application will automatically be abandoned. (e) Nevertheless, the applicant may file a request for postdating of the application. Such a request should be filed before expiry of 12 months period from the date of filing of provisional specification. If the same applicant has filed more than one applications, accompanied by provisional specifications, which are cognate (related) or a modification of one another, the applicant can make a request on plain paper for filing a single complete specification in respect of all such provisional specifications. The complete specification should be filed within the period of twelve months taken from the date when the earliest of these provisional specifications was filed. The complete specification is a techno-legal document which fully and particularly describes the invention and discloses the best method of performing it. Main features of complete specification are: i) The Complete Specification must be framed with utmost good faith and must not contain any false representation or description of the invention or any material part of it, which would otherwise mislead the public. The complete specification must not be framed in ambiguous languages but must be as clear and concise as the nature of the subject would admit. ii) The complete specification must be intelligible to an ordinary workman possessing the ordinary skill and knowledge of that branch or the useful art to which the invention relates. It is not required to describe the invention and the manner in which it is to be performed so fully as to instruct persons wholly ignorant of the subject matter. iii) If the complete specification describes anything, which is not new, it must be clearly distinguished from the novel features of the invention. iv) An amendment by way of modifications and variations of the description if any, must fall within the scope of the description v) If the inventor does not disclose all the relevant information or mislead the public or gives a false description of the invention, the patent would be liable to be revoked. vi) The detailed description should be supplemented by drawings in all cases in which the inventions are capable of being illustrated. vii) It is not enough if a mere list of the various parts that make up the apparatus or device is given. The mode of construction of the apparatus and the function of its different parts should be described.

The following documents are to be attached along with complete specification:

a) Statement and Undertaking regarding foreign filing details in respectof same invention (Form 3),

b) Declaration as to Inventorship (Form 5) : In case of a convention application, PCT National Phase application and when complete specification is filed after provisional. It should be filed within one month from the date of filing.

The Following Types of Applications for Patent can be Filed

Ordinary Application

An application for patent filed in the Patent Office without claiming any priority of application made in a convention country or without any reference to any other application under process in the office is called an ordinary application. Such an application can be filed by an inventor himself (as an applicant) or by a person to whom the invention is assigned by the inventor (an assignee is the applicant), without claiming any priority of application made in a convention country or without referring to any other application being processed in the Patent Office. The applicant can be either from India or from abroad.

Convention Applications

When an applicant files the application for a patent, claiming a priority date based on the same or substantially similar application filed in one or more of the convention countries, it is called a convention application. In order to get convention status, an applicant should file the application in the Indian Patent Office within twelve months from the date of first filing of a similar application in the convention country. The convention application is where a person has made an application for a patent in respect of an invention in a convention country (basic application in his own country), and that person or the legal representative or assignee of that person makes an application under this Act for a patent within twelve months after the date on which the basic application was made, the priority date of a claim of the complete specification, being a claim based on matter disclosed in the basic application, is the date of making of the basic application. Where applications for protection have been made in one or more convention countries in respect of two or more inventions which are cognate or of which one is a modification of another, a single convention application be made in respect of those inventions at any time within twelve months from the date of the earliest of the said applications for protection, provided that the fee payable on the making of any such application shall be the same as if separate applications have been made in respect of each of the said inventions. The **priority document and its verified English translation** also should be submitted by the applicant. A convention application shall be accompanied by a complete specification.

When two or more applications for patents constituting one invention have been made in one or more convention countries, one application may be made within twelve months from the date on which the earlier or earliest of those applications was made. Multiple fees has to be remitted for claiming multiple priorities, so that other applications filed earlier in the convention countries, will be deemed to have been published in India. An applicant of convention application shall furnish when required by the Controller, the copies of specification or documents (priority documents) certified by the official chief of the patent office of the convention country.

PCT International Application and PCT National Phase Application

PCT is an international filing system for patents in which the applicant gets an international filing date in all the designated countries, conferring the late entry (up to 31 months) to the national offices without affecting the priority date. This is a simple and economical procedure for the applicants seeking protection for their inventions in many countries. Indian Patent Office is a Receiving Office for international applications by nationals or residents of India. An international application shall be filed with the appropriate office under rule 4 in triplicate either in English or in Hindi language. An international application, made according to the Patent Cooperation Treaty, designating India can enter national phase within 31 months from the priority date of international application or date of filing of international application whichever is earlier. Such an application filed before the Controller in the Indian Patent Office claiming the priority and international filing date is called PCT national phase application. Applicant can enter national phase with a request made in Form 1. The title, description, drawings, abstract and claims filed with the application shall be taken as the complete specification for the purposes of filing in India. The filing date of the application shall be the international filing date accorded under the Patent Cooperation Treaty. Although it is obligatory on the part of International Bureau of WIPO to send pamphlets to the designated offices for convenience and faster processing, the applicant shall submit the necessary documents in duplicate upon entry into national phase. The Patent Office may ask for any other documents, which are necessary in addition to what was submitted along with the application. Certified copies of the priority documents are to be filed within 3 months from the date of communication from the Patent Office. The procedure described under PCT involves two steps of processing the international application. The "International Phase" deals with conducting the search and allowing the applicant to amend the claims, if required. It also optionally deals with the international preliminary examination. Thereafter, the applicant has to enter the national phase (within the prescribed time limits). The grant of patent is the task of the designated / elected offices, that is, the national offices or regional offices. Under the PCT system, by the time the international application reaches the national / designated office, it has already been searched by the International Searching

Authority and possibly examined by an International Preliminary Examining Authority, thus providing the national Patent Offices with the important benefit of reducing their work loads since they have the benefit of these international phase centralized procedures and, thus, need not duplicate those efforts. Further, objectives of the PCT are to facilitate and accelerate access by industries and other interested sectors to technical information related to inventions and to assist developing countries on gaining access to technology.

Application for Patent of Addition

Patent of addition is filed for a patent in respect of any improvement in or modification of an invention described or disclosed in the complete specification filed. The Controller may, if the applicant so requests, grant the patent for the improvement or modification as a patent of addition. A patent is not granted as a patent of addition unless the date of filing of the application was the same as or later than the date of filing of the application in respect of the main invention. A patent of addition shall not be granted before grant of the patent for main invention.

When an applicant feels that he has come across an invention which is a slight modification of the invention for which he has already applied for/ or has patent, the applicant can go for patent of addition since the invention does not involve a substantial inventive step. It is also possible to convert an independent patent to a patent of addition at a later date if the subject matter was an improvement in or modification to a main invention for which he holds a patent. There is no need to pay separate renewal fee for the patent of addition during the term of the main patent. A patent of addition expires along with the main patent unless it is made independent according to the provisions in Section 54. However a patent of addition will not be granted unless the date filing of application was the same or later than the date of filing of the complete specification in respect of the main invention. It should be noted that a patent of addition will not be granted before granting of the patent for the main invention.

Divisional Application

When an application made by applicant claims more than one invention, the applicant on his own or to meet the official objection may divide the application and file two or more applications, as applicable for each of the inventions. This type of application, divided out of the parent one, is called a Divisional Application. The priority date for all the divisional applications will be same as that claimed by the Parent Application (Ante-dating). The Complete Specification of a divisional application should not include any matter not in substance disclosed in the complete specification of the first application. The reference of parent application should be made in the body of the specification. A divisional application has to be filed before the grant for a Parent application.

4.2 Publication

No application for patent shall ordinarily be open to public before the publication by Patent Office. At the end of 18 months period, the application will be published in the official journal.

Early Publication: If the applicant makes a request in Form 9 (before the expiry of 18 months from the date of priority if no priority claimed from the date of filing) with the prescribed fee (Rs.2,500/- for natural person(s) and Rs.10,000 for legal entity, the application will be published within one month from the date of filing of such request.

4.3 Request of Examination

No application for a patent shall be examined unless the applicant makes a request in the prescribed form for such examination within the prescribed period. A request for examination on Form 18 along with the prescribed fees within forty-eight months from the date of priority of the application or from the date of filing of the application, whichever is earlier; or within six months from the date of revocation of the secrecy direction, whichever is later; should be submitted so that the application is taken up for examination. The examination process includes: (a) whether the application and the specification and other documents relating thereto are in accordance with the requirements. (b) whether there is any lawful ground of objection to the grant of the patent. (c) the result of investigations made under section 13; and 145 (d) any other matter which may be prescribed. Further the period within which the Controller shall refer the application and specification and other documents to the examiner in respect of the applications where the request for examination has been received shall ordinarily be one month from the date its publication or one month from the date of the request for examination whichever is later. A first examination report along with the application and specification shall be sent to the applicant or his authorised agent ordinarily within six months from the date or the request for examination or six months from date of publication whichever is later. The time for putting an application in order for grant under shall be twelve months from the date on which the first statement of objection is issued to the applicant to comply with the requirements.

A list of objections made by the examiner will be communicated to the applicant in the First Examination Report (FER). A FER along with the application and specification is sent to the Applicant or his Authorized Agent ordinarily within six months from the date of request for examination or six months from the date of publication, whichever is later? If any of the objections require amendment of the application to ensure compliance with the provisions of the Act or the Rules, the same will be communicated to the applicant along with the FER. The applicant will be allowed to carry out the necessary amendments of the application. The amended documents along with the superseded pages, duly marked, cancelled and initialled by the applicant or his agent will be returned to the Controller. Copies of any pages that have been added or retyped and any drawing that has been added or substantially amended shall be submitted in duplicate. The amended documents together with the specification will be examined again in the same way as the original specification. The applicant will be given an opportunity of being heard, if he so requests, when the examination report is adverse to him and he contests any of objections or re files his specification along with his observations regarding amendments of the same.

The request for such hearing should be made at least 10 days before the expiry date. There can be one or more correspondences after the issue of FER. However, the time for meeting the objections and putting the application in order for grant is 12 months from the date of issue of FER, failing which the application will be abandoned.

Post Dating of The Application

The application for patent can be post-dated to a date not later than six months from the date of application on a request made by the applicant at any time before the grant of patent along with the prescribed fee as given in first schedule. However this provision will not apply if the application is deemed to be abandoned. If the application or specification (or drawings if any) is amended to comply with the requirements of the Act or the Rules and the Controller feels that post-dating is required, he may direct that application or specification or other documents related thereto be deemed to have been made on the date on which the requirements are complied with or the date on which it is re-filed after complying with the requirements.

Pre-grant Opposition

Pre grant opposition can take place when Complete Specification does not sufficiently And clearly describe the invention or when Complete specification does not describe the method by Which the invention is to be performed, Non-disclosure or wrongful mentioning of source and Geographical origin of biological material OR **Subject matter** does not constitute an 'invention' under Section 2 (1) (j) and lack of Inventive step / non obvious, Industrial application and Claims. When Invention frivolous / contrary to natural laws, Contrary to public order / morality, Prejudice to human / animal / plant life Or health or environment. Mere discovery of a scientific principle or abstract theory or discovery of any living thing or non-living Substances occurring in nature or mere discovery of any new property / mere new use For a known substance / mere use of a known Process, machine or apparatus Substance obtained by a mere admixture resulting only in the aggregation of the properties or a process for producing such Substance. The mere arrangement or re-arrangement or duplication of known devices each functioning independently, Method of agriculture / horticulture, Process for the medicinal / surgical / curative / prophylactic Diagnostic / therapeutic / other treatment of human beings or any process for a similar treatment of animals, plants and animals in whole or any part thereof including Seeds, varieties and species / essentially biological processes. Computer programme per se other than its technical application to Industry or a combination with hardware, Mathematical method / business method / algorithms, Literary, dramatic, musical or artistic work or any other aesthetic creation including cinematographic works and television productions, mere scheme or rule or method of performing mental act, method of playing game, a presentation of information, topography of integrated circuits, traditional knowledge or an aggregation or duplication of known properties of traditionally known components. **Novelty or** Invention anticipated by prior publication, prior claiming, Claim (s) of conflict(s) with claim (s) of (c) Invention claimed in claim (s) prime facie lacking in novelty, specification not clearly worded, claims define a plurality of distinct inventions, each claims relates to an independent invention.

4.4 PCT Application: Gateway to Foreign Patents

The Patent Cooperation Treaty (PCT) is an agreement for international cooperation in the field of patents. It is the most significant advancement in international cooperation in this field since the adoption of the Paris Convention itself. It is, however, largely a treaty for rationalization and cooperation with regard to the filing, searching and examination of patent applications and the dissemination of the technical information contained therein. The PCT does not provide for the grant of "international patents". The task and responsibility for granting patents remains exclusively in the hands of the Patent Offices of, or acting for, the countries where protection is sought (the "regional Offices"). PCT is a special agreement under the Paris Convention open only to states, which are members of the Paris convention and is administered by International Bureau (IB) under World Intellectual Property Organization (WIPO), Geneva.

The procedure described under PCT involves two steps of processing the international application. The "International Phase" deals with conducting the search and allowing the applicant to amend the claims, if required. It also optionally deals with the international preliminary examination. Thereafter, the applicant has to enter the national phase (within the prescribed time limits).

The grant of patent is the task of the designated / elected offices, that is, the national offices or regional offices. PCT is an international filing system for patents in which the applicant gets an international filing date in all the designated countries, conferring the late entry (up to 31 months) to the national offices without affecting the priority date. This is a simple and economical procedure for the applicants seeking protection for their inventions in many countries. Indian Patent Office is a Receiving Office for international applications by nationals or residents of India. An international application shall be filed with the appropriate office under rule 4 in triplicate either in English or in Hindi language. An international application, made according to the Patent Cooperation Treaty, designating India can enter national phase within 31 months from the priority date of international application or date of filing of international application whichever is earlier. Such an application filed before the Controller in the Indian Patent Office claiming the priority and international filing date is called PCT national phase application. Applicant can enter national phase with a request made in Form 1. The title, description, drawings, abstract and claims filed with the application shall be taken as the complete specification for the purposes of filing in India. The filing date of the application shall be the international filing date accorded under the Patent Cooperation Treaty. Although it is obligatory on the part of International Bureau of WIPO to send pamphlets to the designated offices for convenience and faster processing, the applicant shall submit the necessary documents in duplicate upon entry into national phase. The Patent Office may ask for any other documents, which are necessary in addition to what was submitted along with the application. Certified copies of the priority documents are to be filed within 3 months from the date of communication from the Patent Office. When an applicant feels that he has come across an invention which is a slight modification of the invention for which he has already applied for/ or has patent, the applicant can go for patent of addition since the invention does not involve a substantial inventive step. It is also possible to convert an independent patent to a patent of addition at a later date if the subject matter was an improvement in or modification to a main invention for which he holds a patent. There is no need to pay separate renewal fee for the patent of addition during the term of the main patent. A patent of addition expires along with the main patent unless it is made independent. However a patent of addition will not be granted unless the date filing of application was the same or later than the date of filing of the complete specification in respect of the main invention. It should be noted that a patent of addition will not be granted before granting of the patent for the main invention.

Chapter - 5

Patent Bodies

5.1 TRIPS

TRIPS (*Trade Related Aspects of Intellectual Property Rights*) is an international agreement facilitated by World Trade Organization (WTO) that sets down minimum standards of many forms of Intellectual Property (IP) regulation. It reduces distortions and impediments to international trade, and promote effective and adequate protection of intellectual property rights ensuring that measures and procedures to enforce intellectual property rights do not themselves become barriers to legitimate trade; It helps in: the applicability of the basic principles of GATT 1994 (*General Agreement on Tariffs and Trade)* and of relevant international intellectual property agreements or conventions; (b) the provision of adequate standards and principles concerning the availability, scope and use of trade-related intellectual property rights; (c) the provision of effective and appropriate means for the enforcement of trade-related intellectual property rights, taking into account differences in national legal systems; (d) the provision of effective and expeditious procedures for the multilateral prevention and settlement of disputes between governments; and (e) transitional arrangements aiming at the fullest participation in the results of the negotiations. TRIPS recognizes the need for a multilateral framework of principles, rules and disciplines dealing with international trade in counterfeit goods; ensuring that intellectual property rights are private rights and underlying public policy objectives of national systems for the protection of intellectual property, including developmental and technological objectives. It also looks after the special needs of the least-developed country Members in respect of maximum flexibility in the domestic implementation of laws and regulations in order to enable them to create a sound and viable technological base, e*mphasizing* the importance of reducing tensions by reaching strengthened commitments to resolve disputes on trade-related intellectual property issues through multilateral procedures; to establish a mutually supportive relationship between the WTO and the World Intellectual Property Organization (WIPO) as well as other relevant international organizations. The agreement states that 1. Members shall give effect to the provisions of this Agreement. Members may, but shall not be obliged to, implement in their law more extensive protection than is required by this Agreement, provided that such protection does not contravene the provisions of this Agreement. Members shall be free to determine the appropriate method of implementing the provisions of this Agreement within their own legal system and practice. 2. For the purposes of this Agreement, the term "intellectual property" refers to all categories of intellectual property. 3. Members shall accord the treatment provided for in this Agreement to the nationals of other Members. **1.** In respect of the relevant intellectual property right, the nationals of other Members shall be understood as those natural or legal persons that would meet the criteria for eligibility for protection provided for in the Paris Convention (1967), the Berne Convention (1971), the Rome Convention and the Treaty on Intellectual Property in Respect of Integrated Circuits, were all Members of the WTO members of those conventions. **2.** Any Member availing itself of the possibilities provided in paragraph 3 of Article 5 or paragraph 2 of Article 6 of the Rome Convention shall make a notification as foreseen in those provisions to the Council for Trade-Related Aspects of Intellectual Property Rights (the "Council for TRIPS"). TRIPS is related to the **protection** of intellectual property that do not constitute an arbitrary or unjustifiable discrimination against nationals of other Members.

"Protection" includes matters affecting the availability, acquisition, scope, maintenance and enforcement of intellectual property rights as well as those matters affecting the use of intellectual property rights specifically addressed in this Agreement.

5.2 WTO

World Trade Organization

The *World Trade Organization (WTO) is the only international organization dealing with the global rules of trade between nations. Its main function is to ensure that trade flows as smoothly, predictably and freely as possible. The World Trade Organization came into being in 1995. One of the youngest of the international organizations, the WTO is the successor to the General Agreement on Tariffs and Trade* ***(GATT)*** *established in the wake of the Second World War.* So while the WTO is still young, the multilateral trading system that was originally set up under GATT is well over 50 years old. The past 50 years have seen an exceptional growth in world trade. Merchandise exports grew on average by 6% annually. Total trade in 2000 was 22-times the level of 1950. GATT and the WTO have helped to create a strong and prosperous trading system contributing to unprecedented growth. The system was developed through a series of trade negotiations, or rounds, held under GATT. The first rounds dealt mainly with tariff reductions but later negotiations included other areas such as anti-dumping and non-tariff measures. The last round -the 1986-94 Uruguay Round- led to the WTO's creation. The negotiations did not end there. Some continued after the end of the Uruguay Round. In February 1997 agreement was reached on telecommunications services, with 69 governments agreeing to wide-ranging liberalization measures that went beyond those agreed in the Uruguay Round. In the same year 40 governments successfully concluded negotiations for tariff-free trade in information technology products, and 70 members concluded a financial services deal covering more than 95% of trade in banking, insurance, securities and financial information. In 2000, new talks started on agriculture and services. These have now been incorporated into a broader agenda launched at the fourth WTO Ministerial Conference in Doha, Qatar, in

November 2001. The WTO has about 150 members, accounting for about 95% of world trade. Around 30 others are negotiating membership. Decisions are made by the entire membership. This is typically by consensus. A majority vote is also possible but it has never been used in the WTO, and was extremely rare under the WTO's predecessor, GATT. The WTO's agreements have been ratified in all members' parliaments. The WTO's top level decision-making body is the **Ministerial Conference** which meets at least once every two years. Below this is the **General Council** (normally ambassadors and heads of delegation in Geneva, but sometimes officials sent from members' capitals) which meets several times a year in the Geneva headquarters. The General Council also meets as the Trade Policy Review Body and the Dispute Settlement Body. At the next level, the **Goods Council, Services Council and Intellectual Property (TRIPS) Council** report to the General Council. Numerous **specialized committees, working groups** and **working parties** deal with the individual agreements and other areas such as the environment, development, membership applications and regional trade agreements. The WTO Secretariat, based in Geneva, has around 600 staff and is headed by a director-general. Its annual budget is roughly 160 million Swiss francs. It does not have branch offices outside Geneva. Since decisions are taken by the members themselves, the Secretariat does not have the decision-making role that other international bureaucracies are given. The Secretariat's main duties are to supply technical support for the various councils and committees and the ministerial conferences, to provide technical assistance for developing countries, to analyze world trade, and to explain WTO affairs to the public and media. The Secretariat also provides some forms of legal assistance in the dispute settlement process and advises governments wishing to become members of the WTO.

5.3 WIPO

The World Intellectual Property Organization (WIPO)

The World Intellectual Property Organization (WIPO) is one of the specialized agencies of the United Nations (UN) system of organizations. The "Convention Establishing the World Intellectual Property Organization" was signed at Stockholm in 1967 and entered into force in 1970. However, the origins of WIPO go back to 1883 and 1886, with the adoption of the Paris Convention and the Berne Convention respectively. Both of these conventions provided for the establishment of international secretariats, and both were placed under the supervision of the Swiss Federal Government. The few officials who were needed to carry out the administration of the two conventions were located in Berne, Switzerland. Initially there were two secretariats (one for industrial property, one for copyright) for the administration of the two conventions, but in 1893 the two secretariats united. The most recent name of the organization, before it became WIPO, was BIRPI, the acronym of the French-language version of the name: United International Bureaux for the Protection of Intellectual Property (in English). In 1960, BIRPI moved from Berne to Geneva. At the 1967 diplomatic conference in Stockholm, when WIPO was established, the administrative and final clauses of all the then existing multilateral treaties administered by BIRPI were revised. They had to be revised because member States wished to assume the position of full governing body of the Organization (WIPO), thus removing the supervisory authority of the Swiss Government, to give WIPO the same status as all the other comparable intergovernmental organizations and to pave the way for it to become a specialized agency of the United Nations system of organizations. Most of the intergovernmental organizations now called specialized agencies did not exist before the Second World War. They were created for the specific purpose of dealing with a particular subject or field of activity at the international level. However, some intergovernmental organizations, such as the International Labor Office (ILO), the Universal Postal Union (UPU) and the International Telecommunication Union (ITU) were in existence, and had become the responsible intergovernmental organizations in their respective fields of activity long before the establishment of the United Nations. After the United Nations was established, these organizations became specialized agencies of the United Nations system. Long before the United Nations was established, BIRPI was the responsible intergovernmental organization in the field of intellectual property. WIPO, the successor to BIRPI, became a specialized agency of the United Nations when an agreement was signed to that end between the United Nations and WIPO which came into effect on December 17, 1974. A specialized agency, although it belongs to the family of United Nations organizations, retains its independence. Each specialized agency has its own membership. All member States of the United Nations are entitled to become members of all the specialized agencies, but in fact not all member States of the United Nations are members of all the specialized agencies. Each State decides for itself whether it wants, or does not want, to become a member of any particular specialized agency. Each specialized agency has its own constitution, its own governing bodies, its own elected executive head, its own income, its own budget, its own staff, its own programs and activities. Machinery exists for coordinating the activities of all the specialized agencies, among themselves and with the United Nations, but basically each agency remains responsible, under its own constitution, to its own governing bodies, which are the States members of the organization. The agreement between the United Nations and WIPO recognizes that WIPO is, subject to the competence of the United Nations and its organs, responsible for taking appropriate action in accordance with its basic instrument and the treaties and agreements administered by it, *inter alia,* for promoting creative intellectual activity and for facilitating the transfer of technology related to industrial property to developing countries in order to accelerate economic, social and cultural development.

Mission and Activities

The mission of WIPO is to promote through international cooperation the creation, dissemination, use and protection of works of the human mind for the economic, cultural and social progress of all mankind. Its effect is to contribute to a balance between the stimulation of creativity worldwide, by sufficiently protecting the moral and material interests of creators on the one hand, and providing access to the socio-economic and cultural benefits of such creativity worldwide on the other. WIPO's place on the international scene has greatly changed since its beginnings, when it was created to serve as the secretariat of treaties concluded between States. Although WIPO has maintained this function (it currently administers 23 such treaties), together with the consequential one of promoting intergovernmental cooperation in the administration of intellectual property, its activities have not only expanded, but also got diversified. An outstanding example of the expansion of WIPO's earlier work is the growth of its registration activities, the increase in the use of international treaties that create the facility of a single procedure to apply for patents and register trademarks and industrial designs, valid in up to all States party to those treaties. The Patent Cooperation Treaty (PCT), the Madrid Agreement and Protocol Concerning the International Registration of Marks, and the Hague Agreement Concerning the International Deposit of Industrial Designs have all given rise to an increased volume of registration activities. To strengthen this aspect of WIPO's work, a new international treaty, namely, the Patent Law Treaty, came into existence in June 2000: its purpose is to streamline application procedures and to reduce the cost of obtaining simultaneous patent protection in several countries. In its more recent history, WIPO increasingly does not stop short of promoting all kinds of intellectual property. This is only the means to achieve an end, which is to promote human creativity that results in industrial and cultural products and services enriching human society as a whole. Thus WIPO is increasingly involved in helping developing countries, whose creativity has yet to be adequately harnessed, to receive the full benefits of the creations of their citizens, as well as those of the outside world. WIPO's role is to assist them also in the preparation and enforcement of laws, in the establishment of sound institutions and administrative structures and in the training of appropriate personnel. WIPO has given particular attention to the 49 Least Developed Countries (LDCs), and has also given similar assistance to countries whose economies are in transition, in Central Asia, Central and Eastern Europe and the Baltic region. WIPO's cooperation for development program is closely interwoven with governmental and intergovernmental cooperation, including WIPO's agreement with the World Trade Organization (WTO), whereby WIPO assists developing countries in the implementation of WTO's Agreement on Trade-Related Aspects of Intellectual Property Rights (TRIPS) The problem of development is compounded by rapid technological and scientific progress. WIPO's approach is twofold: it is to identify and to promote international solutions to the legal and administrative problems posed by digital technology, especially the Internet, to the traditional notions and practices of intellectual property. WIPO's work in alternative dispute resolution between individuals and companies, through the WIPO Arbitration and Mediation Center has been extended to cover the problems arising from the misuse of domain names on the Internet. WIPO has been accredited by the Internet Corporation for Assigned Names and Numbers (ICANN) to administer cases filed under ICANN's Uniform Domain Name Dispute Resolution Policy. Disputes are handled and resolved online, enabling parties to settle cases in a time- and cost-effective manner, without being physically present in the same place. A project that will greatly advance the sharing of valuable intellectual property information benefits is the worldwide global intellectual property information network (WIPONET), a project launched by WIPO in 1999. WIPONET is designed to establish a secure, global network linking the intellectual property offices of all WIPO's Member States, facilitating access to and exchange of information worldwide. Already WIPO's main and subsidiary websites are heavily used all over the world. WIPO is increasingly adopting a global approach not only to intellectual property in itself, but to the place of intellectual property in the wider framework of emerging issues such as traditional knowledge, folklore, biological diversity, environmental protection and human rights. WIPO has followed the method of consultation and empirical research to find, for example, the relation between intellectual property and genetic resources, traditional knowledge and folklore. One of the most significant present-day tasks of WIPO is to demystify intellectual property, so that it is recognized as a part of everyday life not only by those directly involved in it at governmental, legal, industrial and cultural levels, but also by any others who compose civil society, whether in non-governmental organizations or small businesses, whether farmers, public health personnel, individual creators or simply interested members of the general public. WIPO's activities aim to give to all levels of society an awareness of how they have a stake in a healthy intellectual property system, and also to provide them with access to the knowledge, experience and expertise that will enable them to use those systems effectively.

5.4 Paris Convention

The Paris Convention for the Protection of Industrial Property

As a follow-up to the Vienna Congress, an International Congress on Industrial Property was convened at Paris in 1878. Its main result was a decision that one of the governments should be asked to convene an international diplomatic conference "with the task of determining the basis of uniform legislation" in the field of industrial property. Following that Congress, a final draft proposing an international "union" for the protection of industrial property was prepared in France and was sent by the French Government to a number of other countries, together with an invitation to attend the 1880 International Conference in Paris. That Conference adopted a draft convention which contained in essence the substantive provisions that today are still the main features of the Paris Convention. A Conference was convened in Paris in 1883, which ended with final approval and signature of the Paris Convention for the Protection of Industrial Property. The Paris Convention was signed by 11 States: Belgium, Brazil, El Salvador, France, Guatemala, Italy, the Netherlands, Portugal, Serbia, Spain and Switzerland. When it came into effect on July 7, 1884, Great Britain, Tunisia and Ecuador had adhered as well, bringing the initial number of member countries to 14. El Salvador, Guatemala and Ecuador later denounced the Paris Convention to join again in the 1990s. After World War II the Paris Convention increased its membership more significantly. The Paris Convention has been revised from time to time after its signature in 1883. Each of the revision conferences, starting with the Brussels Conference in 1900, ended with the adoption of a revised Act of the Paris Convention. With the exception of the Acts concluded at the revision conferences of Brussels (1897 and 1900) and Washington, D.C. (1911), which are no longer in force, all those earlier Acts are still of significance, although the great majority of the countries are now party to the latest Act, that of Stockholm of 1967.

Principal Provisions

The provisions of the Paris Convention may be sub-divided into four main categories:

1. a first category contains rules of substantive law which guarantee a basic right known as the right to national treatment in each of the member countries;
2. a second category establishes another basic right known as the right of priority;
3. a third category defines a certain number of common rules in the field of substantive law which contain either rules establishing rights and obligations of natural persons and legal entities, or rules requiring or permitting the member countries to enact legislation following those rules;
4. a fourth category deals with the administrative framework which has been set up to implement the Convention, and includes the final clauses of the Convention.

5.5 Berne Convention

The Berne Convention for the Protection of Literary and Artistic Works

Copyright protection on the international level began by about the middle of the nineteenth century on the basis of bilateral treaties. A number of such treaties providing for mutual recognition of rights were concluded but they were neither comprehensive enough nor of a uniform pattern. The need for a uniform system led to the formulation and adoption on September 9, 1886, of the Berne Convention for the Protection of Literary and Artistic Works. The Berne Convention is the oldest international treaty in the field of copyright. It is open to all States. Instruments of accession or ratification are deposited with the Director General of the World Intellectual Property Organization (WIPO). The Berne Convention has been revised several times in order to improve the international system of protection which the Convention provides. Changes have been effected in order to cope with the challenges of accelerating development of technologies in the field of utilization of authors' works, in order to recognize new rights as also to allow for appropriate revisions of established ones. The first major revision took place in Berlin in 1908, and this was followed by the revisions in Rome in 1928, in Brussels in 1948, in Stockholm in 1967 and in Paris in 1971. The purpose of the Stockholm revision was to provide for rapid technological developments as well as the needs of newly independent developing countries, and to introduce administrative and structural changes. As for the preferential provisions for developing countries worked out in Stockholm, these were further taken up at the Paris Revision Conference in 1971, where new compromises were worked out. The aim of the Berne Convention, as indicated in its preamble, is "to protect, in as effective and uniform a manner as possible, the rights of authors in their literary and artistic works." Article 1 lays down that the countries to which the Convention applies constitute a Union for the protection of the rights of authors in their literary and artistic works.

Principal Provisions

Basic Principles

The Convention rests on three basic principles. Firstly, there is the principle of "national treatment", according to which works originating in one of the member States are to be given the same protection in each of the member States as these grant to works of their own nationals. Secondly, there is automatic protection, according to which such national treatment is not dependent on any formality; in other words protection is granted automatically and is not subject to the formality of registration, deposit or the like. Thirdly, there is independence of protection, according to which enjoyment and exercise of the rights granted is independent of the existence of protection in the country of origin of the work.

Works Protected

Article 2 contains a non-limitative (illustrative and not exhaustive) list of such works, which include any original production in the literary, scientific and artistic domain, whatever may be the mode or form of its expression. Derivative works, that is those based on other pre-existing works, such as translations, adaptations, arrangements of music and other alterations of a literary or artistic work, receive the same protection as original works. The protection of some categories of works is optional; thus every State party to the Berne Convention may decide to what extent it wishes to protect official texts of a legislative, administrative and legal nature, works of applied art, lectures, addresses and other oral works and works of folklore. Furthermore, Article 2(2) provides for the possibility of making the protection of works or any specified categories thereof subject to their being fixed in some material form. For instance, protection of choreographic works may be dependent on their being fixed in some form. One of the important provisions is the one that covers works or expressions of what is called "folklore." Without mentioning the word, the Convention provides that any member country may give protection to unpublished works where the identity of the author is unknown, but where there is every ground to presume that the author is a national of that country, by designating, through the national legislation, the competent authority which should represent the author of unknown identity and protect and enforce his rights in the countries party to the Convention. By providing for the bringing of actions by authorities designated by the State, the Berne Convention offers to countries whose folklore is a part of their heritage, a possibility of protecting it.

5.6 Budapest Treaty

The Budapest Treaty on the International Recognition of the Deposit of Microorganisms for the Purposes of Patent Procedure

The Budapest Treaty on the International Recognition of the Deposit of Microorganisms for the Purposes of Patent Procedure (the Budapest Treaty), which is a special agreement under Article 19 of the Paris Convention, entered into force on August 9, 1980.

Background to the Treaty

Disclosure of the invention is a generally recognized requirement for the grant of patents. Normally, an invention is disclosed by means of a written description. Where an invention involves a microorganism, or the use of a microorganism, which is not available to the public, such a description is not always sufficient for disclosure. That is why in the patent procedure of an increasing number of countries it is necessary not only to file a written description but also to deposit, with a specialized institution, a sample of the microorganism. Patent Offices are not equipped to handle microorganisms, whose preservation requires special expertise and equipment to keep them viable, to protect them from contamination and to protect health or the environment from contamination. Such preservation is costly. The furnishing of samples also requires specialized expertise and equipment. When protection is sought in several countries for an invention involving a microorganism or the use of a microorganism, the complex and costly procedures of the deposit of the microorganism might have to be repeated in each of those countries. It was in order to eliminate or reduce such multiplication, in order to enable one deposit to serve the purpose of all the deposits which would otherwise be necessary, that the Treaty was concluded.

Summary of the Treaty

The main feature of the Treaty is that a Contracting State which allows or requires the deposit of microorganisms for the purposes of patent procedure must recognize, for such purposes, the deposit of a microorganism with any "international depositary authority", irrespective of whether such authority is on or outside the territory of the said State. In other words, one deposit, with one international depositary authority, will suffice for the purposes of patent procedure before the national Patent Offices (called "industrial property offices" in the Treaty) of all of the Contracting States and before any regional Patent Office (for example the

European Patent Office) which has filed a declaration of acceptance under Article 9(1)(a) of the Treaty. What the Treaty calls an "international depositary authority" is a scientific institution – typically a "culture collection" – which is capable of storing microorganisms. Such an institution acquires the status of "international depositary authority" through the furnishing, by the Contracting State on the territory of which it is located, of assurances to the Director General of WIPO to the effect that the said institution complies, and will continue to comply, with the requirements specified. It will be available, for the purposes of the deposit of microorganisms, to any "depositor" (person, firm, etc.) under the same conditions, that it will accept and store the deposited microorganisms and that it will furnish samples thereof to anyone entitled to such samples but to no one else. The said assurances may be furnished also by certain intergovernmental industrial property organizations. (Article 7(1)(a)). The Treaty and the Regulations contain provisions allowing for what is called a "new" deposit where no samples of the originally deposited microorganism can be furnished, for the termination or limitation of the status of international depositary authority at the will of the Contracting States where the said authority does not, or does not fully, comply with its assumed duties , and for all microorganisms deposited with an international depositary authority to be transferred to another such authority if the former is about to cease functioning as such. They also regulate the contents of the receipt that each international depositary authority is required to issue to the depositor for the deposited microorganism and provide for the testing of the viability of the deposited microorganisms and the issuance of viability statements for the international depositary authority to charge a fee for each deposit, the fee covering the minimum 30 years during which the deposited microorganism must be stored. They also contain provisions related to the applicability of the Treaty to intergovernmental industrial property organizations.

Main Advantages of the Treaty

The Treaty is primarily advantageous to the depositor who is an applicant for patents in several countries. It will save him money because, instead of depositing the microorganism in each and every country in which he files a patent application referring to that microorganism, he can deposit it only once, with one depositary, with the consequence that in all but one of the countries in which he seeks protection he will save the fees and costs that deposits would have otherwise entailed. In most cases, there will be at least one international depositary authority in the country of the depositor, which means that he will deal with an authority which is close to him, with which he can deal in his own language, to which he can pay the fees in his own currency and which he may even know from personal experience.

5.7 Madrid Agreement Marks

The Madrid Agreement Concerning the International Registration of Marks and the Protocol Relating to that Agreement

The system of international registration of marks is governed by two treaties, the Madrid Agreement Concerning the International Registration of Marks, which dates from 1891, and the Protocol Relating to the Madrid Agreement, which was adopted in 1989, entered into force on December 1, 1995, and came into operation on April 1, 1996. Common Regulations under the Agreement and Protocol also came into force on that last date. The system is administered by the International Bureau of WIPO, which maintains the International Register and publishes the *WIPO Gazette of International Marks.* The reason for the much more recent Protocol, following the original Madrid Agreement of 1891 (last amended at Stockholm in 1967), was the absence from the Madrid Union of some of the major countries in the trademark field – for example, Japan, the United Kingdom and the United States of America. The Protocol is intended to make the Madrid system acceptable to more countries. It differs from the Agreement in offering such options as:

- a choice for the applicant, allowing international registrations to be based on national applications and not only on national registrations;

- a period of 18 months, instead of one year, for Contracting Parties to refuse protection, with the possibility of a longer period in the case of a refusal based on an opposition;
- the possibility for the office of a designated Contracting Party to receive, instead of a share in the revenue from the standard fees, an "individual fee" whose amount may not be higher than the fees it charges for national or regional registration or renewal, the said amount being diminished by the savings resulting from the international procedure;
- the transformation of an international registration which is no longer protected because the basic mark has ceased to have effect in the country of origin, international or regional applications in some or all of the designated Contracting Parties, with the filing date, and where applicable the priority date, of the international registration;
- the possibility for the Protocol to be joined not only by States, but in addition by any intergovernmental organization which has an office for registering marks with effect in its territory.

The Functioning of the System of International Registration

An application for international registration (an "international application") may be filed only by a natural person or a legal entity which has a real and effective industrial or commercial establishment in, or is domiciled in, or is a national of, a country which is party to the Madrid Agreement or the Madrid Protocol, or who has such an establishment in, or is domiciled in, the territory of an intergovernmental organization which is a party to the Protocol, or is a national of a member State of such an organization. The Madrid system of international registration cannot be used by a person or legal entity which does not have the necessary connection, through establishment, domicile or nationality, with a member of the Madrid Union. Nor can it be used to protect a trademark outside the Madrid Union. A mark may be the subject of an international application only if it has already been registered (or, where the international application is governed exclusively by the Protocol, if registration has been applied for) in the Office of origin. In the case of an international application governed exclusively by the Agreement or by both the Agreement and Protocol, the Office of origin is the Trademark Office of the Contracting State in which the applicant has a real and effective industrial or commercial establishment; if he has no establishment in such a State, it is the Office of the Contracting Party where he has a domicile; if he has no domicile in such a State, it is the Office of the Contracting State of which he is a national. In the case of an international application governed exclusively by the Protocol, these restrictions on the choice of Office of origin (sometimes referred to as the "cascade") do not apply; the Office of origin may be the Office of *any* Contracting Party with respect to which a person or entity fulfills one or more of the above conditions. An international application must designate one or more Contracting Parties (not the Contracting Party whose Office is the Office of origin) in which the mark is to be protected. Further Contracting Parties may be designated subsequently. A Contracting Party may be designated only if that Contracting Party and the Contracting Party whose Office is the Office of origin are both party to the same treaty, that is, the Agreement or the Protocol.

The designation of a given Contracting Party is made under that treaty which is common to that Contracting Party and the Contracting Party whose Office is the Office of origin. Where both Contracting Parties are party to both the Agreement and the Protocol, it is the Agreement which governs the designation; this follows from the so-called "safeguard" clause, Article 9*sexies* of the Protocol. It follows that there are three kinds of international application:

- an international application *governed exclusively by the Agreement*; this means that all the designations are made under the Agreement;
- an international application *governed exclusively by the Protocol;* this means that all the designations are made under the Protocol;

- an international application *governed by both the Agreement and the Protocol*; this means that some of the designations are made under the Agreement and some under the Protocol.

5.8 The Patent Law Treaty (PLT)

The Patent Law Treaty (PLT) was adopted on June 1, 2000 at a Diplomatic Conference in Geneva. The purpose of the PLT is to harmonize and streamline formal procedures in respect of national and regional patent applications and patents. With a significant exception for the filing date requirements, the PLT provides maximum sets of requirements which the Office of a Contracting Party may apply: the Office may not lay down any additional formal requirements in respect of matters dealt with by this Treaty. Any State which is party to the Paris Convention for the Protection of Industrial Property or which is a member of WIPO may become party to the PLT. In addition, any intergovernmental organization may become party to the Treaty if the following conditions are fulfilled:

(i) at least one of the Member States of the organization is party to the Paris Convention or a member State of WIPO;

(ii) the organization has been duly authorized to become party to the Treaty in accordance with its internal procedures;

(iii) the organization is competent to grant patents with effect for its member States, or it has own legislation binding on all its member States concerning matters covered by the Treaty and has, or has designated, a regional Office for the purpose of granting patents.

Provisions of the Treaty and the Regulations

The Treaty applies to national and regional applications that are applications for patents for invention, applications for patents of addition and divisional applications for patents for invention or for patents of addition. These terms are to be construed in the same sense as the corresponding terms in Article 2(i) of the Patent

Cooperation Treaty (PCT). The PLT also applies to international applications for patents for invention and for patents of addition filed under the PCT once the international applications have entered into the "national phase." It also applies to the time limits for the entry of international applications into the national phase under PCT. As regards patents, the Treaty applies to all patents for invention, and to patents of addition, that have been granted by the Office of a Contracting Party or by another Office on behalf of that Contracting Party.

Filing Date Requirements

The grant of a filing date is essential to deciding who has priority for the grant of a patent in each country and to determining prior art and the patentability of the invention. It is also relevant to claiming a right of priority under the Paris Convention as well as to the calculation of the term of patent protection. Article 5 of the Treaty sets up requirements for obtaining a filing date and procedures to avoid loss of the filing date because of a failure to comply with other formality requirements. In principle, the Office of any Contracting Party shall accord a filing date to an application on the basis of three elements. These are: (i) an indication that what was filed is intended to be a patent application; (ii) indications which identify the applicant and/or allow the applicant to be contacted; and (iii) a part which on the face of it appears to be a description. A Contracting Party may, however, accept evidence that establishes the identity of, or allows a contact to, the applicant in the place of indications referred to in (ii) above, or accept a drawing in the place of a part referred to in (iii) above. Further, for the purpose of obtaining a filing date, an applicant may file a description in any language, although he/she may need to file a translation later.

Chapter - 6

Other Fields of Intellectual Property Protection

6.1 Copyrights

Copyright law is a branch IPR which deals with the rights of intellectual creators. Copyright law deals with particular forms of creativity, concerned primarily with mass communication. It is concerned also with virtually all forms and methods of public communication, not only printed publications but also such matters as sound and television broadcasting, films for public exhibition in cinemas, etc. and even computerized systems for the storage and retrieval of information. Copyright deals with the rights of intellectual creators in their creation. Most works, for example books, paintings or drawings, exist only once they are embodied in a physical object. But some of them exist without embodiment in a physical object. For example music or poems are works even if they are not, or even before they are, written down by a musical notation or words. Copyright law, however, protects only the form of expression of ideas, not the ideas themselves. The creativity protected by copyright law is creativity in the choice and arrangement of words, musical notes, colours, shapes and so on. Copyright law protects the owner of rights in artistic works against those who "copy", that is to say those who take and use the form in which the original work was expressed by the author. Copyright protection is above all one of the means of promoting, enriching and disseminating the national cultural heritage. A country's development depends to a very great extent on the creativity of its people, and encouragement of individual creativity and its dissemination is a *sine qua non* for progress. Copyright constitutes an essential element in the development process. Experience has shown that the enrichment of the national cultural heritage depends directly on the level of protection afforded to literary and artistic works. The greater the number of a country's intellectual creations, the higher its renown; the greater the number of productions in literature and the arts, the more numerous their so-called "auxiliaries" (the performers, producers of phonograms and broadcasting organizations) in the book, record and entertainment industries; and indeed, in the final analysis, encouragement of intellectual creation is one of the basic prerequisites of all social, economic and cultural development.

Subject Matter of Copyright Protection

The subject-matter of copyright protection includes every production in the literary, scientific and artistic domain, whatever the mode or form of expression. For a work to enjoy copyright protection, however, it must be an original creation. The ideas in the work do not need to be new but the form, be it literary or artistic, in which they are expressed must be an original creation of the author. And, finally, protection is independent of the quality or the value attaching to the work—it will be protected whether it be considered, according to taste, a good or a bad literary or musical work—and even of the purpose for which it is intended, because the use to which a work may be put has nothing to do with its protection. Works eligible for copyright protection are, as a rule, all original intellectual creations. A non-exhaustive, illustrative enumeration of these is contained in national copyright laws. To be protected by copyright law, an author's works must originate from him; they must have their origin in the labour of the author. But it is not necessary, to qualify for copyright protection, that works should pass a test of imaginativeness, of inventiveness. The work is protected irrespective of the quality thereof and also when it has little in common with literature, art or science, such as purely technical guides or engineering drawings, or even maps. Exceptions to the general rule are made in copyright laws by specific enumeration; thus laws and official decisions or mere news of the day are generally excluded from copyright protection. Practically all national copyright laws provide for the protection for the types of work as: ***literary works:*** novels, short stories, poems, dramatic works and any other writings, irrespective of their content (fiction or non-fiction), length, purpose (amusement, education, information, advertisement, propaganda, etc.), form (handwritten, typed, printed; book, pamphlet, single sheet, newspaper, magazine); whether published or unpublished; in most countries "oral works," that is, works not reduced to writing, are also protected by the copyright law; *musical works:* whether s erious or light; songs, choruses, operas, musicals, operettas; if for instructions, whether for one instrument (solos), a few instruments (sonatas, chamber music, etc.), or many (bands, orchestras); *artistic works:* whether two-dimensional (drawings, paintings, etchings, lithographs, etc.) or three-dimensional (sculptures, architectural works), irrespective of content (representational or abstract) and destination ("pure" art, for advertisement, etc.); *maps and technical drawings; photographic works:* irrespective of the subject matter (portraits, landscapes, current events, etc.) and the purpose for which they are made; *motion pictures ("cinematographic works"):* whether silent or with a soundtrack, and irrespective of their purpose (theatrical exhibition, television broadcasting, etc.), their genre (film dramas, documentaries, newsreels, etc.), length, method employed (filming "live," cartoons, etc.), or technical process used (pictures on transparent film, videotapes, DVDs, etc.). *computer programs* (either as a literary work or independently). Many copyright laws protect also "works of applied art" (artistic jewellery, lamps, wallpaper, furniture, etc.) and choreographic works. Some regard phonograph records, tapes and broadcasts also as works.

Rights Comprised in Copyright

The owner of copyright in a protected work may use the work as he wishes; but not without regard to the legally recognized rights and interests of others and may exclude others from using it without his authorization. Therefore, the rights bestowed by law on the owner of copyright in a protected work are frequently described as "exclusive rights" to authorize others to use the protected work. The original authors of works protected by copyright also have "moral rights", in addition to their exclusive rights of an economic character. What is meant by "using" a work protected by copyright? Most copyright laws define the acts in relation to a work which cannot be performed by persons other than the copyright owner without the authorization of the copyright owner.

Right of Reproduction and Related Rights

The right of the owner of copyright to prevent others from making copies of his works is the most basic right under copyright. For example, the making of copies of a protected work is the act performed by a publisher who wishes to distribute copies of a text-based work to the public, whether in the form of printed copies or digital media such as CD-ROMs. Likewise, the right of a phonogram producer to manufacture and distribute compact discs (CDs) containing recorded performances of musical works is based, in part, on the authorization given by the composers of such works to reproduce their compositions in the recording. Therefore, the right to control the act of reproduction is the legal basis for many forms of exploitation of protected works. Other rights are recognized in national laws in order to ensure that the basic right of reproduction is respected. For example, some laws include a right to authorize distribution of copies of works. **The right of distribution** is usually subject to exhaustion upon first sale or other transfer of ownership of a particular copy, which means that, after the copyright owner has sold or transferred ownership of a particular copy of a work, the owner of that copy may dispose of it without the copyright owner's further permission, for example, by giving it away or even by reselling it. Another right which is achieving wider and wider recognition, including in the TRIPS Agreement is the right to authorize rental of copies of certain categories of works, such as musical works included in phonograms, audiovisual works, and computer programs. The right of rental is justified because technological advances have made it very easy to copy these types of works; experience in some countries has shown that copies were made by customers of rental shops, and therefore, that the right to control rental practices was necessary in order to prevent abuse of the copyright owner's right of reproduction. A major category of acts restricted by copyright consists of the acts of broadcasting works and of communicating works to the public by means of wires or cables. When a work is broadcast, a wireless signal is emitted into the air which can be received by any person, within range of the signal, who possesses the equipment (radio or television receiver) necessary to convert the signal into sounds or sounds and images. When a work is communicated to the public by cable, a signal is diffused which can be received only by persons who possess such equipment linked to the cables used to diffuse the signal. In principle, according to the Berne Convention for the Protection of Literary and Artistic Works, owners of copyright have the exclusive right of authorizing both the wireless broadcasting and the diffusion by cable of their works.

Piracy and Infringement

The rights of an owner of copyright are infringed when one of the acts requiring authorization of the owner is done by someone else without his consent. The unauthorized copying of copyright materials for commercial purposes and the unauthorized commercial dealing in copied materials is known as "piracy."

Incidence of Piracy

An essential part of piracy is that the unauthorized activity is carried on for commercial gain. This element of commercial gain implies that piracy will often be carried out on an organized basis, since not only is the unauthorized reproduction of a work involved, but also the subsequent sale or distribution of the illegally reproduced work, which will require some form of organized distribution network or contact with potential purchasers. To the consumer, often only the end of the chain of such a distribution network will be visible in the form of one sales outlet selling a pirated product. It is important to bear in mind, however, particularly when addressing the question of the means of dealing effectively with piracy, that behind one such outlet will often lie a systematically organized illicit enterprise, which illegally reproduces a copyrighted work and distributes it to the public via a number of such sales outlets. The first has been the advances in the means by which intellectual works may be communicated. The medium of the printed word has been supplemented progressively by media for communicating audio and visual recordings in the form of phonograms, music cassettes, films and video grams. computer has added a further means of recording and communicating information. Digital technology has had a tremendous impact on the creation, dissemination and use of works.

6.2 Trademarks

A trademark is any sign that individualizes the goods of a given enterprise and distinguishes them from the goods of its competitors." This definition comprises two aspects, which are sometimes referred to as the different functions of the trademark, but which are, however, interdependent and for all practical purposes should always be looked at together. In order to individualize a product for the consumer, the trademark must indicate its source. This does not mean that it must inform the consumer of the actual person who has manufactured the product or even the one who is trading in it. It is sufficient that the consumer can trust in a given enterprise, not necessarily known to him, being responsible for the product sold under the trademark. The function of indicating the source as described above presupposes that the trademark distinguishes the goods of a given enterprise from those of other enterprises; only if it allows the consumer to distinguish a product sold under it from the goods of other enterprises offered on the market can the trademark fulfil this function. This shows that the distinguishing function and the function of indicating the source cannot really be separated. For practical purposes one can even simply rely on the distinguishing function of the trademark, and define it as "any visible sign capable of distinguishing the goods or services of an enterprise from those of other enterprises."

An application for registration of Trade Marks is received at the Head office (Mumbai) in India and its branches according to territorial jurisdiction. Applications are then examined mainly with regard to the distinctiveness, possibility of deceptiveness and conflicting Trade Marks. The registrar on consideration of the application and any evidence of use or distinctiveness decides whether the application should be accepted for registration or not, and if accepted, publishes the same in the official gazette i.e. Trade Marks Journal (published in CD-Rom). Within a prescribed period any person can file an opposition, a copy of which is served to the applicants who is required to file a counterstatement within two months failing which the application shall be treated as abandoned. Thereafter, the opponent leads evidence in support of his case by way of affidavit followed by the applicant's evidence also by way of affidavit in support of the application. After that the opponent files evidence by way of rebuttal. On completion of evidence, the matter is set down for a hearing and the case is decided by a Hearing officer. The registrar's decision is appealable to the Intellectual Property Appellate Board. Almost all functions of the Registry have now been decentralised and executed by respective offices except publication of journal, issuance of Registration Certificate and post registration activities including renewal which is done at TMR, Head Office. The day to day administration of Trade Marks Act,1999 is the main responsibility of the Registry. Apart from the above, the Registry have other functions like offering preliminary advice; providing Official Search Report of same/similar Trade Marks on records for requested goods/services; cause a search to be made for issue a certificate under Section 45(1) of the Copyright Act, 1957 to the effect that no trade mark identical with or deceptively similar to such artist work as sought to be registered as a Copyright has been registered as a Trade Mark; providing to interested public information and guidance on the subject; providing information to various government agencies including Police, Central Excise Personnel, establishment of a Public Grievance and Redressal Cell, maintenance of top class IP library, the production of annual statistical report, production of official Trade Marks Journal in electronic form and submit an Annual Report to Parliament.

Any person claiming to be the proprietor of a trade mark used or proposed to be used by him may apply in writing in prescribed form along with prescribed fee at the Trade Mark office for registration. The application should contain the trade mark, the goods/services, name and address of applicant and agent (if any) with power of attorney, period of use of the mark and signature. The application should be in English or Hindi. It is provided under the Trade Marks Act,1999 that goods and services are classified according to the International Classification of goods and services. Currently **schedule IV** of the Act provides a summary of list of such goods and services falling in different classes which is merely indicative. The Registrar is the final authority in the determination of the class in which particular goods or services fall. The Schedule IV of the Act is annexed at the end of this questionnaire on Trade Marks.

Any name (including personal or surname of the applicant or predecessor in business or the signature of the person), which is not unusual for trade to adopt as a mark. An invented word or any arbitrary dictionary word or words, not being directly descriptive of the character or quality of the goods/service. Letters or numerals or any combination thereof. The right to proprietorship of a trade mark may be acquired by either registration under the Act or by use in relation to particular goods or service. Devices, including fancy devices or symbols, Monograms, Combination of colours or even a single colour in combination with a word or device, Shape of goods or their packaging, Marks constituting a 3- dimensional sign, Sound marks when represented in conventional notation or described in words by being graphically represented.

Trade Marks identify the actual physical origin of goods and services. The brand itself is the seal of authenticity, it guarantees the identity of the origin of goods and services, it stimulates further purchase, it serves as a badge of loyalty and affiliation. It may enable consumer to make a life style or fashion statement.

Benefits from a Trade Marks

The Registered Proprietor of a Trade Marks can stop other traders from unlawfully using his trade mark, sue for damages and secure destruction of infringing goods and or labels. The Trade Marks Registry is expected to earn a revenue of nearly Rs.40 crores during the current year and which is perpetually on the rise. Apart from this the Legal professionals gets huge benefit. The Trade Marks Registration system is driven by professionals and legal and para legal advisors (Agents) who act for the clients in the processing of the trade marks application. The registration of a trade mark confers upon the owner the exclusive right to the use of the registered trade mark and indicate so by using the symbol (R) in relation to the goods or services in respect of which the mark is registered and seek the relief of infringement in appropriate courts in the country. The exclusive right is however subject to any conditions entered on the register such as limitation of area of use etc. Also, where two or more persons have registered identical or nearly similar mark due to special circumstances such exclusive right does not operate against each other. For filing new applications there are prescribed forms depending on the nature of application such as Form TM-1, TM-2, TM-3, TM-8, TM-51 etc. With prescribed **fee of Rs.2,500/-.** To file a Notice of Opposition to oppose an application published in the Trade Marks Journal **(FormTM-5). Fees:Rs.2,500/-,** for Renewal of a Regd. Trade Mark **(Form TM-12). Fees: Rs.5,000.**

6.3 Geographical Indications

Geographical Indications of Goods are defined as that aspect of industrial property which refer to the geographical indication referring to a country or to a place situated therein as being the country or place of origin of that product. Typically, such a name conveys an assurance of quality and distinctiveness which is essentially attributable to the fact of its origin in that defined geographical locality, region or country. Under Articles 1 (2) and 10 of the Paris Convention for the Protection of Industrial Property, geographical indications are covered as an element of IPRs. They are also covered under Articles 22 to 24 of the Trade Related Aspects of Intellectual Property Rights (TRIPS) Agreement, which was part of the Agreements concluding the Uruguay Round of GATT negotiations. India, as a member of the World Trade Organization (WTO), enacted the Geographical Indications of

Goods (Registration & Protection) Act, 1999 has come into force with effect from 15th September 2003. Every application for the registration of a geographical indication should be made in the prescribed form and should be signed by the applicant or his agent and must be made in triplicate along with three copies of a Statement of Case. An application to register a geographical indication for a specification of goods included in any one class should be made in Form GI-1. It must be reasonably practicable for persons inspecting the Register or reading the Geographical Indications Journals to understand from the graphical representation what the geographical indications is. An application for the registration should not be of a three dimensional, unless the application for registration contains a statement to that effect. Where a colour combination is claimed as an element of a geographical indication in an application for the registration, it should not be acted upon as such unless the application contains statement to that effect and specifies the colours. Every application should be in respect of one geographical indications only for as many class or classes of goods as may be made. Some of the examples are: Darjeeling Tea (Type- Agriculture, West Bengal), Chanderi Fabric (Type-Handicraft, Madhya Pradesh), Kotpad Handloom (Type-Handicraft, Orissa), Solapur Chaddar (Type-Handicraft, Maharastra), Blue Pottery (Type-Handicraft, Jaipur). When geographical indications are considered as a special kind of distinctive sign used in commerce and thus as a particular category of intellectual property, it is important to distinguish them from trademarks: whereas a trademark identifies the enterprise which offers certain products or services on the market, a geographical indication identifies a geographical area in which one or several enterprises are located which produce the kind of product for which the geographical indication is used. Thus, there is no "owner" of a geographical indication in the sense that one person or enterprise can exclude other persons or enterprises from the use of a geographical indication, but each and every enterprise which is located in the area to which the geographical indication refers has the right to use the said indication for the products originating in the said area, but possibly subject to compliance with certain quality requirements such as prescribed, for example, in administrative decrees governing the use of appellations of origin.

Protection of Geographical Indications

Protection means the right to prevent unauthorized persons from using geographical indications, either for products which do not originate from the geographical place indicated, or not complying with the prescribed quality standards. The second aspect related to the issue of protection is the question of protecting geographical indications against becoming generic expressions: in that case they have lost all their distinctiveness and, consequently, will lose their protection. The question whether a geographical indication is a generic term and void of any protection is, in the absence of an international agreement, to be determined by national law. It might well be that a geographical name is regarded in one country as a geographical indication and is protected accordingly, whereas it is considered to be a generic or semi-generic term in another country. Examples for such diverging treatment of geographical names are the French names "Champagne" and "Chablis" which, in France, are only allowed to be used for products originating from a certain geographical area and produced according to certain quality standards, whereas, in the United States of America for example, they are regarded as being semi-generic names, and therefore may be also used for wines not originating from the French area of production. This aspect of protection is especially important in the context of international protection of geographical indications and is dealt with, for example, by the Lisbon Agreement for the Protection of Appellations of Origin and their International Registration.

6.4 Trade Secrets

This IPR does not exist in India. A Trade Secret is the secret information about the product or process. It can be any formula, pattern, device or compilation of information which is used in one's business that is treated with confidentiality and which gives the owner of the secret an opportunity to obtain an advantage over competitors. To maintain ownership rights over Trade Secret, the owner must treat the information with secrecy. It only be disclosed to a reliable person. Coca Cola is an example of Trade Secret. Unlike other forms of IPR, Trade Secret cannot be registered publically.

Chapter - 7

Appendix - A
Diagrammatic Presentation of Processes Involved in Obtaining an Indian Patent

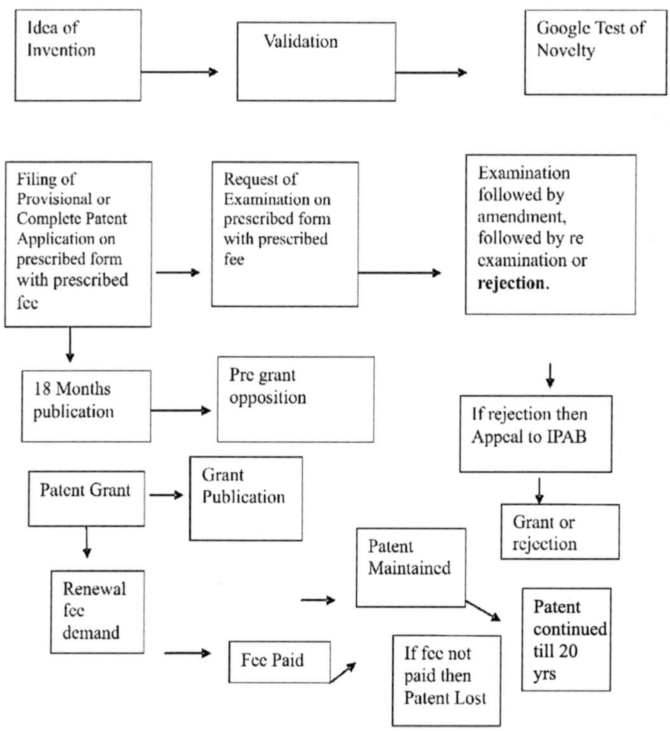

Chapter - 8

Appendix - B
References

1. Introduction IP WIPO
2. International Treaties Patents WIPO
3. Field of IP WIPO
4. Draft Patent Manual 2008, IPO India
5. Enforcement of IP WIPO
6. Role of IP WIPO
7. www. WTO.org TRIPS PDF
8. Role of IP WIPO
9. www.WTO.org